trust ME

RESTORE BELIEF & CONFIDENCE IN AN UNCERTAIN WORLD

LEA BROVEDANI

TRUST ME by Lea Brovedani

BDI Publishers

ISBN 978-1-946637-01-7

FIRST EDITION

Cover & Layout Design: Tudor Maier

BDI Publishers
Atlanta, Georgia

Trust is at the core of any successful organization. Lea Brovedani's *Trust Me: Restore Belief and Confidence in an Uncertain World* is an insightful journey into the world of trust and how it is garnered in corporate America. Businesses assume that their employees and customers trust them but how do they really know? Lea identifies the "Five Tenets of Trust" as a fundamental basis for how leaders should treat others if they are truly interested in establishing a culture of trust that will be recognized both inside and outside their business. I thoroughly enjoyed this book and was impressed that it is void of jargon and is excellent at conveying several critical elements of the trust factor while, at the same time, being entertaining. It is filled with real life anecdotes and stories from both Lea's life as well as informative examples of how others have had to deal with situations that threatened or destroyed the feeling of trust. This is an exceptional leadership book with practical insights and sage advice for both the novice manager and the most seasoned CEO.

Harry Herington, CEO/Chairman
NIC Inc.

The insights that Lea Brovedani shares in her new book are relevant and so timely in this current economic climate. Trust is an essential element in building solid and productive relationships whether it is in the workplace and in life in general. The social fabric of our world is anchored in trust and Lea's formula for building trust works! This book should be a recommended read for anyone in a leadership position.

Paula Morand, 2019 Top 100 Influencer

I have known Lea for 18 years and was so attracted to her way of facilitating and entertaining an audience back then. What was most compelling was how much I believed in everything she said. Not surprisingly, she is now amongst the thought leaders in TRUST. This book has tons of personal stories, principles, anecdotes and a thorough application in business and personal life. Lea gives her position on TRUST in the contemporary business world, the Do's and Don'ts and lets her readers recognize the value TRUST plays in every aspect of our lives. An outstanding book to keep in your library!"

Dr. Granville Ed D'Souza, CEO, CEQ Asia P L
Author of EQ from the Inside Out, Unshakeable Spirit and
EQ for Success and High Performance

Trust is a team building Game-changer!

The five tenants of trust should be THE mandatory ethics lesson for every MBA and TRUST ME – Restore Belief & Confidence in an Uncertain World a must read for CEO's wanting to rebuild a stronger culture of company trust."

Dan Lieven, Managing Partner
Head Room

I am deeply moved by this book. What a wonderful introspection into Trust. I hope my testimonial will be able to adequately convey the importance and the impact this book will have on the lives of those that read it.

Fred Barlow, Vice President & CSO,
Reliance Electric, Inc.

Trust Lea to write a practical, informative, entertaining and thought provoking book on Trust! Her storytelling style makes understanding the value and impact of trust on our professional and personal lives very relatable. A clear reminder, no matter what you do, and where in the world you do it, trust is at the heart of your life's experience. I could somehow identify with every story and feeling described. The follow up questions to her points facilitate creating and focusing your own practice of trust. I share Lea's desire for a more trust filled world.

Liana Bagworth, Founder, Executive Partner,
EQals, Dubai, AER

This book is an amazing collection of stories, lessons and insights on how trust is ultimately the core that drives motivation, engagements, business and personal success. Highly recommended for any leader or person who wishes to embrace trust-building as a way of life to restore belief & confidence in this VUCA world. Lea Brovedani has written a gem of a book on TRUST!

Jonathan Low, CSP PCC CEO Global Success Learning Academy President Global Speakers Federation (2015/2016) 2019 Global Guru Top 30 Hospitality

Contents

To my Dad, Harry Tempest Birkett
Who taught me a lot about trust.

Acknowledgements

If I don't have a deadline, it doesn't get done. That was one of the reasons I hired Helen Wilkie as my book coach. I wanted someone I trusted to give me feedback and perspective on the flow and the stories I included in my book. With an undeniably charming Scottish accent, Helen never held back her comments and suggestions and the book is better because of her. Over the course of the 5 months we worked together I came to see her as a friend.

You may have noticed that Phillip Brovedani did many of the drawings. With a full schedule at university, he still found the time to create many of the illustrations for the book. Although we share the same last name and I take credit for being his mother, I can't take credit for any of his talent. We both recognized that he surpassed my skill at drawing when he was still in primary school.

To all of my friends who offered suggestions and feedback I am forever grateful. From suggesting the title to reading through the first drafts, you made this so much better. I'll be sending you a signed book with all my love and appreciation.

WHY TRUST MATTERS

People don't think about trust until it's gone. Much like money, it isn't important until there isn't any.

In this book, I talk about trust in many areas of life. You'll find stories of personal trust given and broken. You'll also find stories of corporations who have lost trust, often at great costs. Corporations, of course, don't run themselves—They are run by people. Even in huge companies trust issues are about the people.

I grew up with a father who was going to be a millionaire tomorrow but couldn't pay the gas bill today.

He would regale my friends with stories of how he was going to saddle up his horse and head to the hills to find the lost cursed gold mine[1] and retire a rich man.

Maybe the fact that he didn't own a horse and didn't have any money to search for the mine saved him.

I was embarrassed by the tall tales and wanted a Father who was 'normal'.

He was a voracious reader and that fueled his imagination for his inventions. After reading about a small plane that had gone down and couldn't be found, he invented a signal device for downed aircraft based on a timing principle. The man he partnered with to take it to market took off with his money and my father didn't have the finances or the heart to continue.

---

1 Based on the story of the Lost Lemon Gold Mine supposedly worth 7 billion dollars and cursed after one of the miners killed his partner. The money was supposedly hidden and never found.

He had less than a high school diploma but invented complex engineering marvels. Married at 19, by the time he was 24 he had a wife and five children to support. He was a lousy businessman so to keep food on the table he took whatever job he could, always believing that the pot of gold was around the corner and within his reach.

He taught me that contracts couldn't save you if you were working with a dishonest person. That you should get to know someone and always look a person in the eye to see if you could trust them before you did business with them. Like many lessons, he learned them the hard way.

When he died I heard from one person after another that he was always the guy to ask when you needed help. My Dad Harry was trusted to "do what he said he would do."

My work in trust started as a young child as the daughter of Harry Tempest Birkett.

Common Trust Myths Busted

I constantly hear and read long-held beliefs about trust that are frankly wrong.

Here's a quote you've probably heard more than a few times: *We do business with people we know, like, and trust.* The fact is, I do business all the time with people and businesses I don't know. I've sold my coaching services to people who've never met me, and bought things from websites without even talking to another human.

I recently received a new comforter I ordered from an online company called Wayfair. I didn't know them, but they have a glossy website that looked legitimate. Besides, when the parcel arrives at my home, it feels like Christmas. I'm a kid again, with the anticipation of asking for something and hoping I get what I want. Will I or won't I? I know what I ordered, but I'm never really sure it will match the description on the website.

When I ordered this expensive new comforter set, there was no cheery clerk giving me their opinion on the color and quality of the merchandise, no eye contact for me to gauge the sincerity of their words, and no way for me to ask the million-and-one questions I have when purchasing something I have to live with for a few years. I didn't know Wayfair at all, but I was doing business with them.

The second criterion in that oft-used quote is that in order to do business with someone, we must like them. How could I possible like them when I've never met them? I liked the convenience, and the ability to shop in my pajamas, while sipping wine in front of the television, but I really don't think that quote was written with online shopping in mind.

For me, it comes down to being able to measure what I call their *trustability*, and it is the one part of the quote that makes sense. We do business with those we trust!

Here's another trust myth that needs busting: *It takes a lifetime to build trust, and only a moment to destroy it.*

I don't know when this snowball started rolling downhill, but trust isn't lost in one moment. It erodes over time. If trust was lost when we made a mistake, there would be no trust in the world. I love what a colleague, Charles H. Green of Trust Advisors Associates said about this myth:

"If I have a deep level of trust in you, and you screw up a little bit — I'm likely to forgive you, give you another chance, cut you a break. Of course, if you screw up a lot — enough to use up the reservoir of trust we've developed — then that's another matter entirely." — Charles H. Green

15

Trust isn't lost in a moment any more than it's built in a moment. As Charles said, trust isn't a matter of time, it's a matter of quality. If you've built up solid trust over a period of time, it will take more than a momentary lapse to destroy it.

Trust As a Core Value

Speaking at a conference in Malaysia, I asked the audience to share information on their experiences around trust.

First, I asked them to share a time when someone did something that made them feel distrustful towards that person. Suddenly, the room became very animated and loud. I walked around and saw some people with looks of anger and hurt. Some had tears in their eyes as they recalled a moment when someone had broken their trust. One woman shared the story of her brother who had power of attorney over her mother, and had taken all of her money, leaving her with nothing. Another talked of a time when a colleague had taken credit for their work. Another spoke of a cheating spouse. Even though some of these events had happened years before, the sense of betrayal and anger was still evident.

Together we talked about how important trust was and how it felt when it was broken.

There is, however, a second part to the exercise. I asked them to share a time when *they* did something that created distrust. The room turned very quiet. One woman at the front raised her hand:

"Trust is one of my core values. I don't do anything that creates distrust."

Hmmmm. Well, most people don't do things to create distrust. It's an unintentional result of a behavior that usually could have been avoided.

16

This will not surprise anyone, but trust is one of *my* core values. Like most people, I have many values, but my top two are trust and kindness. As part of my certification as a Vital Signs Assessor, helping companies build trust, I underwent a 360 assessment that gave me some surprising news about myself.

A 360 assessment is fittingly titled because it gives a full review from multiple angles. It asks what you believe to be true about yourself, and then asks others to rate you in the same areas. What it doesn't tell you is who answered what. There is no way of finding out how people scored you. Its anonymity allows people to answer without fear of repercussions. It brilliantly shows how people are really feeling about what is happening within the organization and their leadership team.

I contacted 20 people I knew — some long-time colleagues, a few friends, a couple of relatives, and a few new clients who were open to answering some questions. All of their answers were anonymous, so I couldn't find out how anyone scored me or who said what. The tool I used was Leadership Vital Signs (LVS), which provides feedback on five areas and gives an overall score on how well you are trusted.

I'm happy to say that although they are not perfect, my trust scores are all very high. One piece of feedback I received was that I didn't always keep promises, which is a huge trust breaker. I was shocked, but I have to admit it's probably true. I have a busy schedule, and if I don't write something down it's pretty safe to say I might forget it.

I don't know who wrote the comment, and I wish they had felt comfortable coming to me, but it sure had me thinking. What did I promise and forget? Ever had one of those nights when your body is tired but your brain won't shut down? Trying to remember what you forgot is a good way to fry whatever memory you still have!

I took that feedback to heart, and now I make sure I keep **all** my promises, no matter how big or small.

How do you know?

When I interviewed Harry Herington, the highly trusted CEO of NIC, he told me that instead of asking managers, *Do people trust you?* Harry asks, *How do you know people trust you?* He understands that in order for his leaders to be trusted, they have to know what builds trust. He pushes them to find evidence to back up their assumptions about trust.

Harry is onto something. Research on team climate consistently shows that most leaders perceived trust to be a full 40% higher than did the team members. I'm happy to say that the discrepancy between how I scored myself and how others scored me wasn't as high as 40%, but I still scored myself 9% higher than others scored me. There exists a serious misassumption about trust, and Herington's question could help unaware leaders get real.

Let's look at it from a business perspective.

Tony Simons is an associate professor of management and organizational behavior at Cornell University's School of Hotel Administration in Ithaca, New York. He looked at the costs and profits associated with trust.

He surveyed more than 6,500 employees at Holiday Inn Hotels in the United States and Canada. The survey provided questionnaires in the employees' language of choice, and oral surveys to approximately 500 illiterate employees. Workers were asked to rate how closely their manager's words and actions were aligned.

Employees evaluated statements such as: *My manager delivers on promises*, and *My manager practices what he/she preaches*. Once they had completed the questionnaire, they were asked about their commitment to the hotel, and what they felt about the service environment. The questionnaire used statements like *I am proud to tell others I am part of this hotel*, and *My coworkers go out of their way to accommodate guests' special requests*.

When the responses were correlated with the hotels' customer satisfaction surveys, personnel records, and profitability, the results were astounding.

Hotels whose employees strongly believed their managers could be trusted, that their promises were followed through, and they demonstrated their values in action, were substantially more profitable than those when the managers scored average or lower. Even a one-eighth-point improvement in a hotel's score on the five-point scale resulted in an increase in the hotel's profits by 2.5% of the revenues. That translated into a profit increase of more than $250,000 per year per hotel.

So now you've got the picture. Trust is important! Whether it is business trust, societal trust, relationship trust, or interpersonal trust, it can make the difference between success and failure.

It's *that* important.

Chapter 1

WHAT IS TRUST?

How often do you hear the word *trust*? I hear it all the time — in every conversation, every commercial, every TV show — and if it's not said, it's implied. Of course, I know that's because it's a focus for me. I speak and write about trust, so naturally I notice when the word is used. But what exactly *is* it?

"Trust is your willingness to be open, vulnerable, and courageous based on positive expectations." — *Lea Brovedani*

Reputation and *trust* are two words that are often used interchangeably, but there is a big difference. Reputation is a backwards view of what has happened in the past, while trust is forward thinking about what can happen in the future. One affects the other.

If you and I decide to do business together, we are going to check each other's reputations. What are people saying about us? What did we deliver? How quickly do we resolve problems? These days, with a quick online search, we can find out a lot about a person or company's reputation in business by looking at information they post.

I am so grateful that my misspent youth wasn't documented on social media! How many of us would want our reputations based on the mistakes we made in our 20s? I've spent the last 15 years studying and speaking on trust, and the person I am now bears little resemblance to the person I was.

I call my model *The Five Tenets of Trust.* According to the dictionary definition, a tenet is the main principle on which a theory or belief is based.

ten·et

ˈtenət/

noun

The tenets of a theory or belief are the main principles on which it is based.

My Five Tenets of Trust are:

Caring

- Treating people with respect.
- Treating employees as individuals, not commodities.
- Using mistakes as learning opportunities, not weapons.
- Management stands behind its employees and does not "throw people under the bus" when a mistake happens.
- Knowing the personal preferences of clients and staff, and rewarding them accordingly.

Commitment

- Keeping your word no matter what. If it can't be accomplished, asking to be released from the obligation.
- Making commitments to be excellent in all aspects, but firstly knowing what that means, and being able to explain it to others.
- Being committed to open and honest behavior.

21

Consistency

- Ensuring that words and deeds match.
- The organization adheres to a code of conduct.
- Everyone knows the rules.
- The organization stands behind its product and services and provides consistent service.

Competence

- Encouraging continual learning.
- Investing money in quality education.
- Rewarding risk taking.
- Showing employees how to resolve mistakes and never make excuses.

Communication

- Having real conversations, not scripted, phony read-by-the-rule-book ones.
- Communicating in an effective and transparent manner.
- Letters, emails, and voicemails are direct and to the point.
- The first line of communication with staff are emotional face-to-face conversations. (If that is not possible because of distance, then video conferencing or phone conversations)
- Staff treats customers in a reflective manner of how *you* treat *them*.
- Returning calls and letters promptly.
- Admitting mistakes quickly and apologizing .

When all the tenets align and work together, the result is perfect trust.

by Phillip Brovedani

His cartoon so aptly represents what trust is *not*. Trust is both a feeling and an action. You must feel trust, and show it through positive actions.

India

I lived in India from 2011 to 2012. My husband, Ric, was on an assignment that was supposed to last three years. It was shortened to one year — but oh my, what a year! It was a time when I had a chance to write, speak in exotic locales, and take courses that I never previously had the time for. For example, I found the oldest yoga ashram in India and received a yoga certification.

The Yoga Institute of Mumbai spends more time teaching the philosophy of yoga than on the asana or poses we typically

23

associate with yoga. I went in expecting to be able to twist my body into interesting pretzel shapes, and instead came out able to straighten my pretzel brain.

Our class was on the second floor of a room with only overhead fans to cool us. The average temperature on most days was +30°C or over 86°F. When I think of that ashram, I can still hear the *whomp, whomp, whomp* of the fans, and the buzzing of flies.

One particular exercise has stuck with me and still influences me to this day. Our teacher gave us each a variety of different colored lentil beans. She then showed us a picture of a flower we were supposed to replicate using the beans as our medium. Sitting on our mats in either the lotus position or kneeling, we were given as much time as we needed to complete our flower. If we were finished before others we sat quietly and contemplated life — or how freaking hot it was with only a fan to cool us.

When I was finished, I sat back feeling very pleased with myself. My lentil bean flower was something beautiful to behold and I wished I had my phone with me to take a picture.

Our instructor read my delight. She came over and stood over my work of art and me. "Are you happy with what you made?", she asked.

"Yes," I replied. With that she bent down and swiped my beautiful flower with her hand, ruining my design. I stopped myself before I called her a rude name.

She smiled at my look of horror and instructed me to do it again. Now, I don't know about you, but when someone in power destroys my work and tells me to do it again, a lot of doubt sets in. I was feeling confused, insulted, and defiant.

My second flower was even better than the first. Those lentil beans became a thing of beauty and, dare I say, pulsated with life and vibrant color. When I was finished, she approached my mat. I threw myself over my flower, shielding it from the sweep of her hand. I wasn't going to have her ruin this one.

"Did you do your best?" she asked. Without raising my body I assured her that I had.

I don't know how she managed, but she snuck her foot under my arm, and again destroyed my flower. I'm sure my gasp and cuss was heard by everyone in the room.

The lesson that wise teacher taught us is that we do our best in life and once we have completed our part, the outcome is outside of our control. We have to believe and have trust in what we do and then let go.

How many times have you done your best and then couldn't let go of what happened after it left your hands? Letting go can be difficult, but that's how trust is developed.

A Tale of Two Managers

Bill was a manager who stopped for a friendly word with his staff as he walked through the office. He knew how many children each of his employees had — in fact he knew their children by name, and it wasn't unusual to hear something like, "Say Mary, how was Corey's soccer game? Did they make it to the tournament?"

Although he set high expectations for each of his employees, and called them to task if they didn't achieve them, he set even higher expectations for himself. He was always working to be better at everything he did. Anyone who worked for him would tell you, without a doubt that they trusted that he had their best interests at heart, and would follow him anywhere. People felt Bill cared about them and his department had very little turnover.

The other manager, Ted, always arrived before his staff. They knew that when they walked in the door he would already be sitting at his desk working, with his head down and the door closed. At staff meetings he would time everyone's commentary. "I've researched this, and everything that needs to be said can be said in three minutes or less," he would say before anyone even began. If you were still going after four minutes, he would cut you off.

At one meeting, he casually mentioned he would be unable to attend the next week's meeting because he was going on his honeymoon. Until that point, no one had even known whether he was single or married! Someone joked afterwards that they thought he looked happy, but that it's hard to tell if he's a robot. Although people agreed he was efficient, there was nothing warm or friendly about him.

Ted was also well known for his critiques. Belinda, a staff member who had taken a demotion to move from Ted's department to Bill's, explained why.

"I was putting in long hours on a project, and had given up more than one weekend. I was really proud of the work that I had done. When I walked in to Ted's office, he barely looked up and told me to *drop* the work on his desk. His feedback was around a few spelling mistakes. When I asked him what he thought of my suggestions, he said they looked 'good'. Wow, weeks of work and all he could muster was that it looked 'good!"

If you asked anyone on his staff if they trusted him, there was always a long pause followed by a cautious reply, as they looked over their shoulder to see if anyone was listening. One very telling reply I remember was, "We trust Ted to look after Ted".

Staff turnover for his department was higher than the company average. People had been known to turn down good promotions if it meant going to work for Ted.

When we did 360° assessments with Ted's staff (feedback from supervisors, peers, direct reports), he was shocked to find that they didn't trust him. "I pride myself on telling the truth, even when it's unpleasant, so how can they not trust me?"

Ted also said that he really did care about his staff, but he wasn't sure how to show it. Like many people, he thought trust was mainly about truth telling, and honesty was his top core value. They did trust Ted's competence, but they didn't trust that he would defend them, champion them, or even know enough about them to help them reach their goals.

It's not hard to see why Bill was trusted and Ted wasn't.

I've noticed that trusted leaders are usually well liked, as was the former head of a financial institution.

It was the early 90s, and as I was doing a keynote and workshop for their Annual General Meeting, I got to know many of the staff. Even though this was many years ago, this story has always stayed with me.

The person I had most contact with was Donna, the administrative assistant. She told me she had never had a boss she liked and trusted more than her current one.

When I asked her why, Donna told me this story.

The day before her birthday, her boss mentioned that he knew an important day was approaching. She was turning 30. She was pleased that he had remembered, but she knew he made a point of knowing important dates of all the staff, so that wasn't in itself a big deal. He found lots of small ways to show he cared about his staff.

"What do you want for your birthday?" he asked.

Donna said she was sure he expected her to mention something like a ring, a trip, flowers and dinner, or a myriad of other traditional gifts that are usually asked for. He wasn't expecting her to say she wanted a new laundry basket. Donna laughed as she told me.

"I have a young family," she told him, "and we have a ton of laundry. My old laundry basket has fallen apart. I've been looking all over for a hip-hugging laundry basket and haven't been able to find one."

He laughed and said it wasn't what he was expecting, and told her to have a great day.

Donna's desk was on the second floor, overlooking the parking lot. On the day of her birthday, she glanced up and noticed her boss pulling into his regular parking spot. He opened the trunk and pulled out a brand new laundry basket with a big red bow on it. The strange looks he received as he walked across the parking lot didn't seem to faze him.

Upstairs, he came up to Donna and smiled as he placed the gift on her desk. He told her he didn't think anyone would take her seriously about wanting the basket and didn't want her to be disappointed on her birthday.

As she told me the story, a big smile spread across her face. For Donna, there has never been another gift that compares to the gift of the laundry basket from her boss. Not flowers, dinner out or even diamonds. It was the thoughtfulness and the gesture that meant more than any material gift possibly could. Small considerate acts take on huge importance when it comes to building trust.

The Local Bookstore

Have you ever seen the movie with Meg Ryan and Tom Hanks in which Meg Ryan's character owns a wonderful little bookstore?

The movie was called *You've Got Mail.* In the movie, the beautiful little bookstore went out of business because it just couldn't compete with the big chain stores.

In my neighborhood, there is a small local bookstore that reminds me of the one in that movie. Running a successful bookstore is part business acumen, part amazing customer service, and a little bit of magic. Lynn Rosen has all three. She has taken the bold step of opening a store called *Open Book* in the small bedroom community of Elkins Park, and it's doing very well!

On any given day, you will find Lynn's store a hub of activity. She and her staff greet everyone by name and customers always feel welcome. She has gathered writers from all over Philadelphia, and once a month she hosts small, intimate gatherings, where authors read passages from their books and answer questions from readers in the audience.

Lynn and her husband, or someone else she trusts, have carefully vetted every book on every shelf in her store. It always amazes that Lynn can pick up any book, and give me an overview of what it is all about.

Her business has been a success in spite of trends, because Lynn has developed a trusting relationship with people in the neighborhood.

Because of Lynn's store we've started a Christmas tradition in our house. One of the gifts we give our children is a book we hope they will love, and Lynn helped us pick it out. After Christmas dinner and desserts, we light a fire, set out big mugs of hot chocolate, a plate of cookies, and curl up with our new books. For us it's a perfect ending to the day, and I don't think we would have started it without Lynn and her wonderful *Open Book.* If you are in Philadelphia, take the trip to Elkins Park and stop by her store.

Leaving the Business

I have a friend who is an accountant specializing in bankruptcies. He once made the bold statement, "Partnerships don't work".

When I asked him what advice he would give me about starting one, his answer was succinct: "Don't."

That was it. "Don't."

I was asking for his advice around the business I was starting with two friends. The three of us had worked together at a personnel agency, and decided to start our own company combining our expertise, and hopefully keep more of the profits. We had all done really well for other companies, and keeping 90% of the fee rather than 40% was very appealing.

Now, my friend wasn't talking specifically about the business I was thinking of starting. As a forensic accountant, he knew all about bankruptcies, and his experience told him they happened mainly in partnerships. I listened to his stories, but felt we could avoid all of those problems.

We each brought in different strengths. Sally set up the books, and her lawyer husband agreed to write up the partnership agreement for free. That should have been my first red flag.

Linda had an office in her basement, where we could work until we had enough equity built up to lease a downtown office. She loved to party and enjoyed more than an occasional glass of wine. That should have been another red flag.

As I had started the company, I had sketched the logo on a napkin, that eventually found its way onto business cards and stationary. I also brought many loyal customers who were willing to give us vacancies to fill at their companies.

We did so well, that within a year we were able to rent an office in one of the most prestigious buildings in our city, and pay cash for all of the new office furniture.

For a few years we were very successful, but things started to fracture. Linda was struggling with an addiction problem, and was in the midst of a marriage breakup. We never knew what to expect from day to day, and the volatility of her emotions had us all on edge. At the beginning of our partnership we laughed and chatted together, but at the end of our time together the office was quiet, and we only spoke to clients.

I decided to leave the business. I found someone to replace me, thinking that I could have the new person buy me out and everyone would be happy. That's when the fine print in the partnership agreement came out. I was told that she wasn't buying me out of the business, but buying into the business — and they would keep all of the revenue.

After paying lawyers and accountants to unravel the business, I remembered what my friend had told me: "Don't."

I really wish I had listened to him.

Now, I know there are many successful partnerships out there, and my accountant friend's experience with bankruptcies was with the ones that didn't work — like ours. Some of our problems stemmed from poor business practices, but a great many were caused by lack of trust. When problems started to arise, we hid in our offices rather than come out and talk about them.

Reading over my story, I realize that I was culpable as well. I didn't tell them I was leaving until I presented the new business partner for them to consider. As I once heard someone say, "We always believe we're Cinderella, and not the ugly step-sister!" We all grew to distrust each other, and that was our undoing.

Emotions and Trust

The common thread through all these stories is how emotions are related to trust. This is supported by the work of Dr. Jennifer Dunn and Dr. Maurice Schweitzer, of the University of Pennsylvania, and Neuroeconomist, Dr. Paul Zak.

Dunn and Schweitzer conducted experiments to determine the influence of emotional states (happiness, gratitude, anger, pride and guilt) on trust. The experiments confirmed that emotions influence our willingness to trust each other.

They approached random strangers at a train station, and asked them to write down the names of people they knew. Then they asked them to tell a story based on one of the emotions. For example, "Tell me a story about a time in your life when you were really happy." Or "Tell me a time when you were extremely angry, and what happened." They did this for each of the different emotions. They then had the strangers rate the trustworthiness of the people whose names they had written down.

They found that positive emotions increased trust and negative emotions decreased trust, even when the person had nothing to do with creating the emotion.

If we feel anger over a parking ticket, later in the day that feeling is likely to affect how we judge someone's trustworthiness. Even though we believe we are rational, thoughtful individuals, we are a mass of emotions that influence how we behave and trust.

This blows a lot of what we know about trust out of the water. The previous belief was that trust was a combination of our own ability to trust and our knowledge of what we believed to be true of another person (or business).

"This research suggests that we make a decision and use reason to decide whether or not to trust someone." notes Schweitzer.

In other words, trust is made and influenced by irrelevant information. "The extent to which I do or do not trust you is a function not only of how trusting a person I am, and what I know about you, but also a function of irrelevant events that have influenced my emotional state. For example, if I hit a parked car, argued with my spouse, learned that I have to pay a large repair bill (or won an award, had a paper accepted, or saw my stock account grow) beforehand, I would trust you less (or more)."

The main idea in the paper is that emotions influence our ability to trust.

Do you remember a movie called *Wedding Crashers*? Okay, I'm on a movie kick now, so humor me. This movie was about two characters, played by Vince Vaughn and Owen Wilson, crashing wedding receptions, eating and drinking for free, and testing their luck at meeting women. They found that women were a lot more trusting at weddings, and there is science to actually prove it.

When I interviewed Dr. Zak, he told me about his research on what happens to the body when we trust deeply, or are in love.

One of his colleagues was getting married, and agreed to have him set up blood collection to test for oxytocin at the happy event. And yes, I agree that having a tent where people are collecting blood for research at a wedding is a little weird, but it did yield some really interesting insights. The bride had a great sense of humor, and called her wedding "The Vampire Wedding".

The results showed the bride had high levels of oxytocin in her bloodstream, surpassed only by (drum roll please) the brides mother! You thought I was going to say groom didn't you? The groom did have levels of oxytocin in his bloodstream, but it seemed the women in the wedding party outdid him. (oxytocin isn't to be confused with oxycontin, a highly addictive drug, that is a powerful painkiller and popular street drug.)

Dr. Zak discovered oxytocin is released in our blood streams when we are in love and is also present when we trust others.

He also studied the connection between trust and economics, and his work went even further to show the connection between emotions and trust. His conclusion: when trust is strong, the profits soar.

When you understand the components of trust, you can see why there was a difference in the level of trust in the tale of the two managers, and why Lynn and her bookstore are able to succeed where others fail. At the finance company, they trusted Ted to be competent and consistent, but they didn't trust that he had their best interests at heart. He often made them angry and defensive — emotions that destroy trust.

9/11 and Trust

After the 9/11 attacks, I was working on a contract in New York. Flying into the airport felt surreal. Soldiers in full army gear, carrying AK-47s, were checking everyone who came in and out of the airport terminal. Although I remember feeling a little frightened, I felt a strong sense of unity and camaraderie with everyone I met. Strangers were making eye contact and connecting in a way I had never seen in a city that has a reputation for rude indifference.

The taxi I took from the airport dropped me off at the wrong hotel, and the concierge told me my hotel was only a couple of blocks away. It didn't seem worth taking a taxi, so I decided to walk. I never knew two blocks could be so difficult!

There I was, with a briefcase and a suitcase, like a salmon trying to swim upstream, moving on a sidewalk where everyone seemed to be walking in the opposite direction. If you've ever been to New York, you know what I was up against. Sidewalks are

34

packed with people and trying to walk even a couple of blocks with bulky luggage is a big pain. Before 9/11, I would have had a few curse words and dirty looks thrown my way.

On this day, though, a crusty New Yorker with an accent straight out of the Bronx, stopped and asked if I needed help, and walked with me for a short distance to make sure I was headed in the right direction.

Wow! This had never happened to me before in New York, where most people believed you shouldn't trust strangers because they're out to get something. Trust existed between us that day, and it felt good.

It was a small example of what I saw every day of the week I was there. It would seem that empathy and compassion are two emotions that are strongly correlated to trust!

Truth Telling Isn't Part of My Model of Trust

When I'm teaching or speaking at a conference, I often ask people to give me their definition of trust. Inevitably, someone will say, "Trust is about telling the truth."

While I don't, of course, condone lying and deceit, telling the truth is not part of my trust model, largely because the truth is not always clear. I've often seen people think they are telling the truth, when in fact, they are stating opinions and beliefs that may not be true at all.

If truth is based on verifiable facts, we can confirm it by researching the evidence. A **fact** that can be checked out would be: *As of 2013, there have been 57 female astronauts, compared to 477 male astronauts.*

However, if we use this fact as a basis for judgment — such as that women are discriminated against in the astronaut program

— we may no longer be telling the truth. It *may* be true based on the facts, but we can't be sure. It is an **opinion**. We trust people more who share our opinions, and distrust those who don't.

Often, we trust people who share similar beliefs. Unlike an opinion, a belief is based on a person's values, faith or morality. An example of a **belief** based on the astronaut example would be that women shouldn't be allowed in outerspace because they should be home, taking care of their families. Beliefs are usually emotional appeals, that cannot be logically argued.

I know, I might have just geeked out on semantics, but I want you to be able to use this to be as trustworthy as possible. What do you mean by truth? Are you telling a fact, giving an opinion, or spouting a belief when you think you are telling your truth?

Self-Trust

I used to believe that self-trust and confidence were something you were born with. Now, I know they are things you can develop. Before you can trust anyone else, you have to be able to trust yourself first.

Carl Rogers, founder of the Humanistic approach to psychology, talked about the need for unconditional positive self-regard. That doesn't mean you won't continue to improve yourself; however, when you completely accept and love yourself, you open yourself to trusting your instincts and judgments, rather than being controlled by others.

I learned this first hand when I received a gift from my husband that demanded I learn a new skill.

You know that feeling you get when you've been dreaming of something for years and you finally get it? That lovely welling up of gratitude, appreciation, and love! That is what I felt when my husband gave me the Vespa I had always wanted for a milestone birthday. I was excited beyond belief when they delivered it to our house.

"Do you know how to drive this?" the delivery man asked. When I told him I didn't have a clue, and asked him to please give me instructions, I should have realized that five minutes wasn't going to be enough, but he made it look so easy.

After he left, the beautiful teal-green Vespa was sitting in the middle of the driveway, and I decided to move it out of the way. I mean, how hard could it be? I stood beside it, turned the key, hit the throttle full-on, and immediately lost control. My brand new bike, with not even a mile on the speedometer, flipped over on its side and one of the mirrors broke off. The bike was scarred, and so was I.

I was heartbroken — and scared stiff to ride it. The Vespa sat for two years. Yes, two full years. I wanted to drive it, but I lacked confidence. I felt like such a loser. Seriously, it was a scooter, not a Harley, and I was afraid to even sit on it.

I speak at conferences all the time about self-trust, but I didn't connect what I talk about with what was happening within me. The Vespa made me feel incompetent and guilty, and those feelings didn't help build positive trust in myself. I started questioning my ability in other areas. I know this isn't logical, but it's how I felt.

Finally, it was looking at my goals and vision that gave me a wake up call. If I couldn't succeed at this, how could I possibly succeed at bigger goals?

So that summer, heart in hand, I signed up for a motorcycle class. I was a little concerned that I would be the oldest one in the class (I was), and that I would feel out of place and uncomfortable (I didn't).

The rest of the class looked like people who belonged on motorcycles. Although I know there are a lot of investment bankers, lawyers and business people driving Harleys and other motorcycles, none of them were in this group. These people had tattoos, ripped jeans, biker boots, and attitudes.

The weather was ridiculously hot so I came with a cooler, sliced watermelon, and plenty of cold drinks. The motorcycle babes with the tattoos loved me for it. The big guys treated me like their mom, so I liked to think of myself as the Motorcycle Mama! We had bonded, and I was accepted as part of the group — although I'm sure the cold watermelon could take most of the credit.

I had the chance to try out a few different motorcycles, and was equally comfortable on a Honda and a Triumph. By the end of the first day, we were starting our motorcycles and driving them around in a circle. At the end of the week I had a motorcycle license. Whoopee! I was ready.

My husband was pleased. "You're finally going to ride your bike!"

I know you're thinking this is where I tell you I got on the Vespa, drove it 100 miles through a storm, and didn't flinch. That didn't happen. I still felt frightened when I looked at my scooter, even after the time on the motorcycles.

So, the first day I went out and sat on the seat for 10 minutes, and then I walked back inside. The second day I turned the bike on, and sat there without moving it. The third day I drove it to the end of the driveway. It took a full week before I had the confidence to ride it out on the street.

Building self-trust is like learning any new skill. You do it by gaining confidence in doing something well. You do something well by practicing and working at it.

Last year, I traded up to a more powerful Vespa, a 150 SXL. I take it out on the highway, driving at speeds of up to 110 kilometers per hour (that's 68 mph for my American friends). I love the feeling of freedom and excitement. When my husband thinks I'm having a rough day, he suggests that I go for a ride because he knows I'll come back with a big grin on my face.

As my trust in my own ability builds, the distance I travel grows. Isn't that just like life? The self-talk I was giving myself over my Vespa when I was learning how to drive it was brutal, and I would have *unfriended* someone who talked to me like that.

Truly confident people have a lot of self-trust. I'm not talking about false bravado. I'm referring to that quiet confidence exuded by people who know who they are, and are good at what they do.

I've talked to high trust leaders, and asked them: "If you had an important decision to make and your team was telling you to do one thing but your gut and experience told you to go in the opposite direction, what would you do?"

Every one of them told me they would trust their gut. *Every one!*

I asked if they were always right. The answer was no, not always, but most of the time. (Sorry to disappoint you. It would be great if it were 100% fail safe.)

What they did tell me was when they didn't trust their gut and went with others, the outcome was always wrong. Wrong for the company and wrong for them personally.

Measuring trust in Business

They were on the 5th Plant Manager in as many years, and I was brought in, at the HR manager's suggestion, to improve cooperation between   departments. There were too many incidents when work slowed down because departments didn't trust each other, and wouldn't communicate problems that could have been avoided.

If there was a slowdown in production, the common refrain from everyone was "Yes, mistakes happened, but not by our department." No one took ownership of their part in any slowdown, always blaming another departments' failure to communicate.

Turnover wasn't a problem since the company treated employees well, and there weren't many places in the rural area that paid the wages these employees were earning. The HR department tried to recruit people from across the country, and it took months to fill any vacancy.

The HR manager walked me through the plant to help me understand what they did, and showed me the product they made, and sold around the world. From the scientists working in the laboratory to the workers on the machines, each one showed an obvious pride in what they did.

The company depended on their multi million-dollar machines to thoroughly clean the natural product they harvested. The product would gum up the machines, so they had to be taken apart, cleaned, and put back together on a monthly basis. I was told that the machinists were the most valued members of the team.

Without them, the plants would have to be shut down. Luckily for me, the head machinist, Carl, had time to talk to me while his machine was waiting for repair.

Carl wore old denim dungarees over his clothes, that had the distinct imprint of oily handprints. We hit it off immediately. I loved his honest, no B.S. way of talking, and he recognized I respected him, and showed it by listening to what he had to say and being open to who he was without judgment.

Carl was revered for his ability to take apart and fix any of the multi-million dollar machines, and feared for the wicked verbal assaults he unleashed on anyone who got in the way, questioned what he was doing.

At the opposite end of the property, scientists in white coats hovered over beakers and test tubes, looking for new uses for the products they pulled from the ocean. Most of them had Masters degrees and Ph.D.s, and they were quite isolated from the people who worked in the plants. When they were asked how they got along with the rest of the staff, they spoke only of those who worked in their building. They didn't have much connection to the employees who worked in the plant.

Millworkers, machinists, line workers, engineers, accountants, office staff, scientists, chemists — I don't think I've worked with a more varied group.

With weary resignation, the office staff had contact with all of the departments, since they were responsible for paychecks, benefits, and carrying out the Plant Manager's requests.

I decided to use an assessment tool that measured the organizational climate or culture, showing how staff felt about what was happening in the organization. This assessment tool would help create a strategy for working through some of the issues.

Because the assessment was a completely anonymous, people answered honestly, without fearing they would be punished for any negative opinions they gave.

We discovered that the staff did not feel listened to, and felt that the owners and managers talked over them. Although they were highly motivated by their pride in their work and what they were achieving, they didn't feel rewarded for doing anything above and beyond what was required.

Their ability to adapt and innovate was great, but they were discouraged by the constant turnover of managers, and the fact that each one would come in with big promises and a request for doing things differently, which they largely ignored.

Of course, the biggest barrier was the lack of trust between departments. The most effective teams have a strong foundation of trust with others, which results in working collaboratively together.

We had half a day to get everyone together, and it was an interesting dynamic, with more than a few uncomfortable moments. When I brought up the results showing the lack of trust between the departments, they told me I was wrong; that in fact, they all trusted each other. I reminded them that I wasn't giving them my opinion, but simply showing them the results of the survey in which they had participated. It's hard to argue with the facts and evidence.

Since the changes needed to come from them, I was working to get them to come up with the strategies for change. Do you know the sound of crickets? Well, that's what I heard for a few minutes.

Then something wonderful happened. Carl said that he wanted to spend time with the engineers, a department that he had been openly criticizing. There was a look of incredulity on everyone's face. I could have kissed him.

Very often this is all it takes. One person steps up, and there is a domino effect that makes others do so as well.

Trust isn't something you can force. It develops when people get to know each other and listen to each other, as Carl was willing to do. They already trusted his competence, but that one small act opened the door to better relationships. We worked for the rest of the time we had on each of the issues that had been uncovered in the climate survey.

Years later, I'm happy to see that the company is thriving, and although the work we did together was only one small part, it was a significant one.

Chapter 2

TRUST AND MISTRUST IN THE CORPORATE WORLD

The High Cost of Low Trust

It began as a regular travel day for Canadian musician, Dave Carroll, and his band, Sons of Maxwell, back in 2008. They were on their way from Halifax, Nova Scotia to a gig in Omaha, Nebraska. Dave had been told he couldn't bring his prized Taylor guitar onboard as carry-on but had been assured it would be handled with care in baggage.

The flight from Halifax to Omaha was via Chicago, and it was here that things took a downturn. While waiting to deplane to catch his next flight, he heard a woman sitting at the window across the aisle say, "Oh my God, they're throwing guitars out there." These are words no musician wants to hear!

Dave tried reporting the incident to three different United Airlines employees, and each one gave him a variation of the message, "Not my problem." There was nothing for him to do but wait until he got to Omaha and check it out as soon as he could.

When he was finally able to get his guitar and open the case, he was devastated to find that his cherished Taylor guitar, valued at $3,500, had been badly damaged.

Despite his best efforts, and patience beyond anything most of us could muster, Dave was not only unsuccessful in getting compensation from United Airlines, but he was emphatically told that his file was closed and they wouldn't accept any more arguments. Frustrated, Dave privately vowed that he would not give up, but he wouldn't let it get nasty. He would remain respectful to everyone he encountered.

Now, if Dave had been a lawyer, he probably would have sued, but since he was and is a talented songwriter, he wrote a song called, "United Breaks Guitars". In his final call, he told the representative from United that he would write three songs about his experience, create a YouTube video, and he wouldn't stop until he had over one million views. When he posted it on YouTube in July 2009, more than a year after the incident, it went viral with 150,000 views the first day — and as of January 2019 has had over 18 million views.

That's an awful lot of people tapping their feet and singing along with the saga of United's underwhelming passenger service! (You can check out the original video at https://www.youtube.com/watch?v=5YGc4zOqozo

Because of the notoriety of the video, and subsequent publicity, the company eventually offered to pay for the broken guitar, but it was too little too late. According to a Harvard University case study, the cost to United Airlines in lost share price and lost business has been reported to be anywhere from 11 million to 180 million, instead of the $1200 Dave was originally willing to settle for.

It didn't end there. Dave went on to write a book about his experience, and has become a sought-after speaker on the subject of customer service. United uses the videos as part of their customer service training, but you have to wonder if the company will ever be able to recover the trust it lost through one incident; one that could have been avoided if it had done the right thing to begin with.

Dave would tell you *it isn't the mistake that causes distrust, but how the mistake is handled.*

Mistakes happen. I've had experiences where companies have handled them quickly and compassionately and my trust has grown. If United had corrected their mistake immediately, they would have saved themselves millions of dollars — but then we wouldn't have a catchy song and Dave might be performing to smaller audiences!

When trust is low, it takes longer to complete business transactions. We take more time checking and double checking information, strategies and suggestions.

Story of Wells Fargo

A number of friends who know of the work I do in trust sent me the link to a Wells Fargo ad. In the ad, the company is telling the public that they understand they've lost trust, and they are working to rebuild it.

People suggested it was a great ad for me to use in my workshops and on stage, when I'm speaking at conferences. I agree, but for different reasons. They see it as an example where trust was broken and acknowledged, and the company is looking to rebuild.

My reasons are slightly different. You can't break trust for a number of years and think a PR campaign will repair all the damage. *Sorry* doesn't cut it.

Wells Fargo has had a culture of encouraging sales at any cost. They set overly aggressive sales targets that sales associates said were impossible to meet. For over five years, this created a culture that encouraged dishonesty. Employees were told to meet their targets and it didn't matter how they got there. As a result, they created false accounts in customers' names to meet these unattainable goals, and show a success that didn't exist.

45

In all, over 1.5 million fraudulent bank accounts were opened, and half a million unrequested credit cards were authorized.

When they were found out, it resulted in over $1 billion in fines and the firing of the CEO. The penalties came from the Consumer Financial Protection Bureau and the Office of the Comptroller of the Currency, two government agencies tasked with policing financial institutions and keeping them honest.

Wells Fargo's new campaign slogan is *"Building better every day"*. Their ad is beautifully done, and starts with an image of a stagecoach riding across the prairie. The stagecoach is the logo for Wells Fargo, and invokes an image of a bygone era when they were the most trusted financial institute in America.

Here is what they say in the ad:

We know the value of trust. We were built on it.
Back when the company went west for gold, we were the ones who carried it back east.
By steam.
By horse.
By iron horse.
Over the years, we built on that trust.
We always found the way — until (and here the screen goes black for a moment)
We lost it.
But that isn't where the story ends.
It's where it starts again, with a complete recommitment to you.
Fixing what went wrong.
Making things right, and ending product sales goals for branch bankers, so we can focus on your satisfaction.
We're holding ourselves accountable to find and fix issues proactively, because earning back your trust is our greatest priority.
It's a new day at Wells Fargo, but it's a lot like our first day!
Wells Fargo. Established 1852.
Reestablished 2018.

People will hear what you say and watch what you do to see if they align. "Sorry" without behavior that demonstrates you are sincere just doesn't cut it.

Trust Across America – Trust Around the World

I spoke with Barbara Brooks Kimmel, CEO and cofounder of Trust Across America – Trust Around the World, about some of the ads corporations have released in an effort to rebuild lost trust with the public.

Barbara is a no-nonsense person, who sees through deception, and is not afraid to call people on their behavior. She is also an award-winning communications executive, who has built a program that holds people and businesses to a high standard of trust.

She made a comment that stuck with me.

"I'm leery of companies whose first step in rebuilding trust is to hire a publicist or crisis management company, instead of working on the conditions that created the distrust in the first place."

I agree with Barbara. Trust isn't something that can be bought. It is earned through integrity and behavior that shows trust in action. I can understand hiring a publicist, especially if you are a company that relies on customers for your livelihood, but it shouldn't be the only thing you do. If you want to build a trustworthy company, you have to take a hard look at what caused the breach and lost the trust in the first place, and make a commitment to do the work.

This is why Wells Fargo was a great example.

The FACTS®Framework is a tool Barbara co-created to rank and measure the trustworthiness of over 1500 US public companies

47

on five quantitative indicators of trust. When Barbara and I spoke, she pointed me to an analysis she had done using the FACTS®Framework, which included Wells Fargo. Wells Fargo scored lowest in the analysis of the four banks she compared. (To learn more go to *https://www.trustacrossamerica.com*)

Here is the FACTS®Framework.[2]

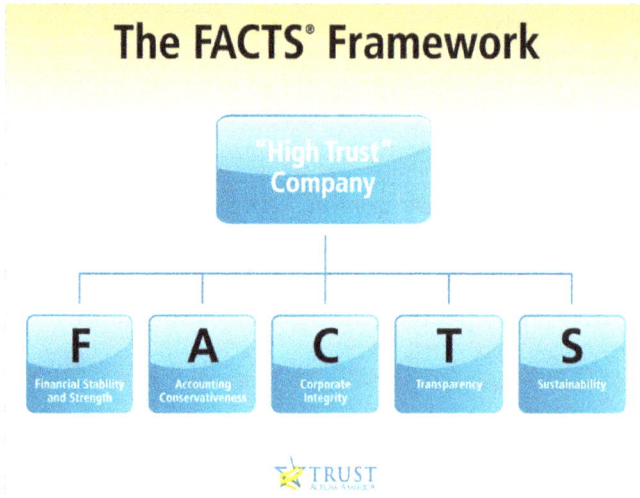

The FACTS® Framework

Wells Fargo isn't the only example of corporate malfeasance by big companies. There are plenty of examples of bad behavior by corporate executives, finding ways to hold on or increase their earnings at all costs.

Facebook and data collection agency, Cambridge Analytica, used information from more than 50 million Facebook users to target ads in the 2016 U.S. election. In 2014, a researcher created an online personality quiz, which users could only get when they agreed to allow the program to collect information on themselves and their friends. The information was forwarded to Cambridge Analytica, who took that information, and created targeted ads for the election. People were not aware that they were being manipulated, and Cambridge broke trust by lying repeatedly about it, until they were finally caught with irrefutable evidence.

2 Reprinted with permission. Copyright 2019, Next Decade, Inc.

Look at many of the pharmaceutical companies in North America, and you'll see examples of corporate greed that boggle the mind. Here's one:

My friends were out at the lake with their young daughter, and her friend, when the young girl screamed that a bee had stung her. If you've ever had a bee sting, you can understand why she screamed — they hurt like heck. In her case it was terrifying, since she was allergic to bee stings, and within minutes she started to go into shock. Luckily she had her EpiPen ® with her, and they were able to inject her.

The EpiPen® is an injection device that contains the drug epinephrine, a chemical that opens airways in the lungs and prevents death in people who have potentially lethal allergic reactions.It didn't take long for it to work, and there was no serious long-term effects. Not everyone is as lucky as my friend's daughter, who has great healthcare coverage, and can afford to have her EpiPen® with her at all times. I get heart palpitations thinking of what could have happened. I always wonder if the people who only consider profit over people ever think of the consequences for less fortunate allergy sufferers.

I don't believe everything that pharmaceutical companies do should be altruistic, but they are in the business of saving lives. and shouldn't that factor into decisions? The makers of the EpiPen® increased the cost of their life-saving injection device by 500%, placing profit over lives, by making it out of reach for many who need it to save their lives. In doing so, they showed they didn't care about people, which breaks the "Caring" tenet of trust.

So yes, I 100% agree with Barbara: if you want to make significant changes, you have to look at the culture of the organization.

Measuring Organizational Trust

When it comes to corporate dysfunction, the problems that surface are just the tip of the iceberg. It's what is going on below the surface that needs to be addressed. Instead of mouthing platitudes and meaningless apologies, there is a way you can actually do something. You might be surprised by what you find.

To measure and improve organizational culture, I use a tool called Organizational Vital Signs (OVS). In Chapter One, I told you about a client who was having trust issues. It was hard to measure trust because people were afraid to voice their real opinions out loud. This tool gave them the anonymity to do so without fear. It allowed us to figure out why they couldn't keep good people in the top management position. What employees told HR wasn't really how they felt, but OVS finally unlocked the truth.

It goes beyond measuring staff satisfaction and looks at critical employee behaviors such as communication, problem-solving and accountability. Once you know where the challenges are, you can create a strategy that works, because it's based on the needs and opportunities for development, not on the perceived problems that might be the tip of a very large iceberg.

Building Trust through Emotional Intelligence

When you look back over these stories you can see the five tenets of trust in action.

As I explained in Chapter One, the five tenets of trust are: caring, commitment, consistency, competence and communication. Since trust is an action as well as a feeling, there is an emotional intelligence component to trust that you see in the tenets.

Caring – Demonstrating genuine care of others

Commitment – Keeping your word or not stopping until your work or task is completed

Consistency – Keeping your words and actions aligned. The rules apply to everyone

Competence – Having a skill or knowledge that aligns with the task

Communication – Being able to listen and verbalize for complete understanding

In all of the stories in the book, you'll see that one or more of the tenets were broken, or completely missing. See if you can identify which of the tenets either positively or negatively was at play.

Warren Buffett and Trust

Warren Buffet is Chairman and CEO of Berkshire Hathaway. According to Business Insider, he is worth $84 billion, and is the third richest man in the world.

Everything I've read about Warren Buffett talks about how he does business with a handshake deal because he is known for his integrity and honor, and being able to access that in others. On a TV interview with Piers Morgan, he said this about his handshake deals:

"You can't make a good deal with a bad guy regardless of any piece of paper. I prefer to do business with people that I like."

Buffet shows that when trust is low, it takes longer to complete business transactions, and there's no guarantee that it won't fall apart. You have to take more time checking and double-checking information, strategies and suggestions.

Just a little aside. If you make a handshake deal with me and walk away from it, what are the consequences? I'd have to decide whether or not to hire a lawyer, take you to court, or at least try you in the court of popular opinion. If you walk away from a handshake deal with the third richest man in the world, do you think the consequences might be different?

I'm sure that anyone who does a handshake deal with a powerful man like Warren Buffett is smart enough to know that breaking trust with him would be a very, very bad idea. I don't want to make him sound like Tony Soprano, but I wouldn't want to test his power.

My experience with a handshake deal didn't go well. I was working as the manager of a recruiting firm in Denver, and I was recruited by a recruiter from another recruiting firm. (Hmmmm, sounds like a Dr. Seuss poem.)

I knew most of the other recruiting firms and relationships were always congenial, so I wasn't surprised when Hal Green called when he was in town, and asked me to go to dinner. We had both started out with the same firm in Calgary, Alberta and it was nice to meet with a friend from my old hometown.

The restaurant we went to was one of the best in the city. It didn't take long for Hal to put the offer before me. It was substantially more than I was currently making, and had a lot of perks. I was wined and dined, and my ego was definitely being stroked.

After a couple of hours I said "Hal, we have a deal. I'd love to head up your operation in Denver. Put together a contract, and I'll sign it."

Hal was no Warren Buffett, but he used the "handshake" deal to close. He told me that if I really trusted him I shouldn't need a contract, and if I did, there was no sense in working together. I like Hal a lot as a friend, but that comment seemed strange to me, and didn't feel right. I ignored my gut, and a big red flag was waving in the back of my mind. I was swayed by the lovely meal, and the dollars that were put in front of me.

The next day I handed in my notice to my company. In the recruiting business, as soon as you give your notice you are asked to leave so that you can't take any files with you. While I was there we were struggling trying to find qualified staff, but I took up the slack, and worked as a manager and recruiter. I found out later that when I left, they had more money going out than what was coming in, and they decided to close their doors.

I loved my new office. The furnishings looked like they were out of a Wall Street law office, and I had a view that overlooked the mountains and downtown Denver. Leaning back in my chair, I looked around and felt that I had made it. I had 20 people reporting to me, and I was younger than all of them. Any guilt I felt over leaving the other company was quickly assuaged by the opulence of my new digs and the power I felt while running the company.

Less than two months into the new job, I tried to use my card to get out of the parking garage and it didn't work. That's when I found out the firm was out of business. The attendant told me parking hadn't been paid for a couple of months-- just about the time I was hired. I called Hal, who admitted that the company had been in trouble for a while. He knew they would be closing the office, but needed someone to bridge the next two months until they could collect the revenue on the deals that were in progress.

My willingness to overlook all the double-dealings was explained in a book by Dan Ariely, called *The (Honest) Truth About Dishonesty*. Dr. Ariely is the James B. Duke Professor of Psychology and Behavioral Economics at Duke University. His book shows how we can be influenced by gifts and praise. In my case, the expensive dinner and the generous salary overrode my reason, and I was willing to leave my job on short notice to join Hal. Dr. Ariely shows that when your willpower is worn down, you are more likely to give in to your desires, and your honesty and integrity can suffer. It was a hard lesson for me to learn, but then, some of the best lessons often are.

I'm not saying you should never do a handshake deal, but for it to work, there has to be honesty, and our deal was a lie from the start. Be honest with yourself, and don't let your own self-interest overrule your reason. I still do some business without a contract, but I go in asking questions, and with my eyes wide open.

Chapter 3

WHAT BREAKS TRUST?

DWYSYD

One important aspect of keeping and maintaining trust is DWYSYD, or *Do What You Say You'll Do*.

I learned early, on as a parent, that if I said we were going to the playground, in my children's eyes I had made a sacred promise, and I had to do what I said I'd do. I've discovered we don't really change that much.

But It's Not Hawaii

I was working as a recruiter for a firm where the profits at the end of the year were double what had been forecasted. The President of the company told us that if we did as well as he was hoping, he was going to take everyone to Hawaii for our Christmas party.

December came, and we were excited, anticipating our exotic holiday with drinks on the beach and warm, sunny days. Then came the announcement that they had decided it just wasn't financially feasible, and instead we were going to a beautiful resort outside of the city. The food and accommodation was all 5-star luxury.

On the evening of the party, the mood in the room was very flat. The usually loud and boisterous group was quiet. Ed announced that he was disappointed in the lack of gratitude the staff exhibited for the party, rooms and meals he was paying for. One of our star performers said, "If we hadn't been promised Hawaii, this would have been appreciated more."

Most of us were gone within six months. We didn't leave because he didn't take us to Hawaii. It was just that Ed consistently over-promised and then dialed back on his promises, and we just got tired of the constant B.S.

Do What You Say You'll Do is possibly the cardinal rule of trust. Break it and trust is gone.

Back in Chapter 1, I talked about Dr. Dunn and Dr. Schweitzer's research on emotions and trust. Simply put, positive emotions fuel trust, and negative emotions deplete it. Does that mean that you are supposed to hide bad news from your staff if you want them to trust you? What about if you are told by management to deliver a message that you don't whole-heartedly agree with?

This is where your communication skills come to the fore in building trust. You have to be a master communicator when delivering both good and bad news. If people don't trust you to give them the straight goods when things are going badly, they probably won't believe you when you're giving them good news either.

Delivering News - The Good, The Bad, and the Ugly

How you deliver news can mean the difference between trust built and trust broken.

The Good News

It's the best news you've heard for a long time — but will everyone see it that way? Most of us love to deliver good news but you need to ask yourself if it's good news for all concerned. You might be thrilled at the latest acquisition, but how will it impact all your staff? That new account you've just landed? What impact is that going to have on the workloads? Are you hiring more people or expecting people to do more work?

Whether you are a big or small company, create a communication plan that answers these questions:

- Who are the people who need to know the information, and who is the best person to deliver the news?

- How relevant is it to the people who are going to receive it?

- Do you have all of the critical information to give them, so they don't have to come back again and again to "fill in the blanks"?

- Who needs to know first?

- How do you want to deliver the message — in person, by phone, by email, by company newsletter?

- When is the best time to deliver it?

According to Forbes, we see an average of 4000-10,000 pieces of information in a day. That is a lot of information coming at us. So when you are communicating, you have to be seen and heard through the noise.

The Bad News

Trust and credibility are vitally important when we are in a crisis. If you want people to trust you, they have to believe you are capable of managing the crisis, and that takes effective communication.

I remembered how I felt when I heard my nephew, whom I had known and adored since the day he was born, was up in Fort McMurray when there was a huge fire in 2016. To give you an idea of the size of the fire, it burned an area larger than the state of Delaware, or more than twice the size of England. It started burning in May of 2016, and was finally deemed to be out in August of 2017.

The city was on fire, and we were waiting for him to be evacuated. Facebook was our connection to him. "Are you safe?" I asked him, as I watched videos of ashes and burning embers raining down on cars and people. He assured us he was safe.

"What about your company? Are they arranging transportation? What have they told you?" I asked.

"I'm very disappointed with my company. There is no information on what we're supposed to do. No information on anything! So I guess we sit and wait."

What?! These were people who were concerned for their lives, and they weren't getting any information.

I've had conversations with Matt since then, and he told me that he doesn't hold fault with any of the people he reported to. The fact that the company didn't have a communication plan was the main problem, and this was exacerbated by the fact that the people who were supposed to communicate had families of their own in the danger zone.

Matt was in a company camp-away from the big fires, so he didn't feel like he was in danger. In fact, he wanted to be evacuated so he could make his room available to the families who needed to be evacuated from the danger zones.

But the truth is that many companies failed miserably at communicating, and trust was lost.

The trust winners, if you can say anyone was a winner in such a sad situation, are the companies that had a communication plan, stepped in and took care of their people. Those companies are looked upon favorably for the work they did during a time of crisis.

I've spoken at conferences about crisis communication, and my first message on the subject is this: **The time to make a communication plan is not *during or after* a crisis**. It should be done, evaluated, and ready to dust off whenever it is needed. I'm sure no one at my nephew's company was expecting a catastrophic fire, but they should have had a plan for any kind of emergency evacuation.

Dr. Peter M. Sandman[3] a crisis communication expert, has six strategies that must be kept in mind during crisis communication. All of this makes perfect sense, and will increase trust.

1. **Don't over-reassure.** Over-reassurance pushes ambivalent audiences toward the alarmed side of the seesaw; it diminishes credibility and leaves them alone with their fears. If you have to get it wrong, it is better to err on the alarming side.

2. **Acknowledge uncertainty.** Sounding more certain than you are rings false, sets you up to be wrong, and provokes debate with those who disagree. Better to say what you know, what you don't know, and what you are doing to learn more. Model the ability to bear uncertainty, and take action anyway.

3. **Treat emotions as legitimate.** In a crisis, people are entitled to be fearful and miserable. Both emotions are at risk of flipping into denial, or escalating into terror, depression, or receding into apathy. To help us bear our feelings, respect our feelings.

---

3 Reprinted with permission from Dr. Peter M. Sandman

4. **Establish your own humanity.** Express your own feelings — if you seem fearless, you can't help but model how others should master fear. Express your wishes: "I wish we could give you a more definite answer." Tell a few stories about your past, your family, your reactions to the crisis.

5. **Offer people things to do.** Self-protective action helps mitigate fear; victim-aid action helps increase misery. All action helps us bear our emotions, and thus helps prevent denial. When possible, offer a choice of actions, bracketing your recommendations with less and more extreme options.

6. **Stop worrying about panic.** Panic is rare. Efforts to avoid panic — for example, by withholding bad news and making over-reassuring statements — tend to backfire. People sometimes disobey in a crisis, but that's not panic. Worry about denial, worry about apathy; don't worry about panic.

These six strategies should be part of every crisis communication. Are they part of yours?

The Ugly News

What happens when you are a manager who has to deliver news you don't agree with? You may be caught in the middle between the staff who report to you and the boss you report to.

When this happens, there are things you can do prior to delivering the message that will make it more credible, and less difficult to deliver. Know how the decision was made, and who was consulted in the making of the decision. Explain to your boss that you know there will be plenty of questions, and you want to understand all aspects of the situation, so you're giving the correct information. Seek the rationale behind the decision. In some cases, you may find that the "C" suite didn't have all of the information, and it may change the decision. Say to your boss "Here are some of the questions they are going to ask", and list them so they have a heads up.

Expressing to your boss all your questions and concerns might even have an impact on the decision that is being made. Also talk to HR, they may know who will be affected and how they will be impacted.

As my seventh grade teacher, Mrs. Hyslop, used to say, "It's not what you say: but how you say it that counts". Practice what you are going to say, and how you are going to say it. Practice your delivery and watch your body language. If you go in with slumped shoulders, mumbling your words, and not making eye contact, you're going to be sending a very mixed message. Even if this is a setback for the staff, there should be no ambivalence in your delivery, and no opportunity for misunderstanding.

Be kind and caring, but don't sugar coat the message. Since you've taken the time to find out all the reasons, you can share these with the staff but don't give them grist for the gossip mill by telling them you disagree with the decision. That helps no one, including you, and doesn't make it easier for them to accept what is happening. If you disagree, let the people who made the decision know your feelings, but don't share them with your staff.

Give people an opportunity to talk and ask questions, and be prepared with the answers. Know the steps the company took before making the decision. People are usually more accepting if they understand the process it took to get to this point.

Trust and the Online Business

The company Wayfair has had quite a bit of business from me since my original leap into the unknown of online shopping with them. I started out ordering small items, but as my trust in them grew I decided to order a large rug for our bedroom. The idea of having it delivered, instead of struggling home with it in the car, was really appealing.

From the moment I hit send on the order, I was impressed and reassured with all the checks and balances they put in place to keep me informed. I knew where my package was at every step of its journey, from the manufacturer to the warehouse, to the delivery van. From my perspective as the trust architect, everything they did built trust.

Finally, the day arrived for the rug to be delivered. Ric and I weren't going to be home, but I knew that wouldn't be a problem, because they could leave it in our enclosed porch. It had been raining every day for the past week, and I was glad the package would be inside so we wouldn't have to worry about water damage.

Then Ric called. "Don't come in the back gate. Park in the driveway. I'll explain when you get home. And by the way, the rug was delivered." He didn't sound pleased.

The rug *had* been delivered, but rather than put it in the porch, the delivery person had thrown it over the fence into the backyard. When Ric came home from the office and opened the electric gate, the rug got caught on the hinges and ripped them out of the wood. The rug, although wrapped in plastic, was lying on the very wet pavement and I couldn't tell if it had also been damaged.

I thought: Why would they would throw the rug onto the wet driveway when it could have been delivered to a dry porch? Instead, they backed the truck up to the gate and, without getting out of the truck, threw it over the fence, and saved themselves time and energy. Placing it on the porch took more work.

I thought of that line, "*It takes a lifetime to build trust, and only one moment to destroy it,*" and wondered if it would be proven right or wrong. That would depend on what happened next.

When I called Wayfair's customer service I was pretty upset. The first person I spoke to followed a script pretty closely.

"I'm so sorry you've had this experience. I'd be upset too."

That did help to calm me, a little, but I wanted to see if they would fix the problem. The person I talked to listened without interrupting, and I was feeling pretty good until they said, "This is a delivery problem with FedEx. We'll give you the number to get in touch with them."

I hadn't hired FedEx to deliver the package. I bought the rug through Wayfair, and I wanted the company I had agreed to do business with to fix the problem, so I asked to speak to a manager.

The manager listened, and told me what she was going to do to correct the situation. Although it was a problem with the delivery company, she did all the paperwork, contacted them, and gave me the name of the person from FedEx who would be calling me.

The next day, she followed up to make sure I had been contacted. The manager from FedEx called and apologized, and also let me know they had been in touch with the delivery driver, and used this as a "teaching moment".

The customer service manager, Janet, made sure I unwrapped and checked the rug from top to bottom to ensure there was no water damage. She told me if I wasn't completely happy they would have someone pick it up, and there would be no charge for the return.

Both companies, FedEx Ground and Wayfair, acknowledged the problem and fixed it. Due to their positive response to my complaint, my trust was restored.

If your company does business online, you need to be sure you go the extra mile, both with the original service and on any complaints you receive, in order to hold the trust of your customers.

Facts, Opinions and Trust

There is a saying I heard when I lived in Halifax, Nova Scotia that went something like this: *"They're blowing warm air up your kilt."* It means the person is telling you what you want to hear in order to make you feel good, instead of what you need to hear.

If you want people to trust you, save the warm air for drying the dishes, and honor people enough to give them the facts.

If you have concerns with someone, whether it's a colleague, direct report, boss, or friend, take the time to write them out. Separate the facts from the beliefs or opinions. Remember, a fact can be verified. If ten different people tell you the facts, they should align.

My son, who is an artist, would tell you everyone interprets a picture differently. What you can rely on is the description of what is on the canvas (the facts). How you feel, and how you interpret the painting is very different for everyone (the belief or opinion).

Take a sheet of paper, and make two columns. On one side, write a fact. On the other side, write an opinion or belief you formed from that fact.

FACTS	OPINIONS OR BELIEF
1. When Bert was talking you inter- rupted three times	-You have no respect for Bert -You think Bert's ideas are ridiculous -You have a tight schedule and needed to speed things up.
2. I spent four hours on Saturday writ- ing a report	-I am dedicated and hard working. -I'm overworked -I have poor time management skills.
3. The boss walked out of the room when I started my presentation	-They don't believe my work is impor- tant, and I should look for another job. -They got a text and had an emergency they couldn't avoid. -I'm not a priority in the organization. -My boss is a jerk.

As you can see, there are lots of ways to interpret actions, and the only way you can find out for sure is to ask. Sometimes, it can be difficult to tell the facts and opinions apart from one another.

It gets even more complicated when we buy into the biases that have been handed down by our parents, teachers and friends. It's one of the reason's I don't have "truth" as part of my trust model, because what is said to be the truth may really be an opinion or a belief.

Learn from the Past

"Learn from the mistakes of others. You can't live long enough to make them all yourself." — **Eleanor Roosevelt**

I sometimes feel I am the only one who has proven Eleanor Roosevelt wrong, as I've made a lifetime of mistakes in my time on the planet. I feel that way until I talk to others, and realize that quite a few people feel the same way I do. If we are willing to, we *can* learn as much, or more, from the hard lessons of others, and avoid making them all ourselves, saving us heartache and pain.

People get emotional when they tell me their story of broken trust. For many, the sense of betrayal and outrage is still palpable after many years.

Stories of Broken Trust, and What We Can Learn from Them

Julie's Story

"I began working for a small therapy business that provided physical, occupational, speech, and play therapy for children from birth to seven years of age. I signed on as a play therapist as an independent contractor, and would visit the office at end of the day, once a week, to drop off invoices.

"The owners were a married couple; both physical therapists. I didn't really get to know any of the other 25 employees, except for the secretary. My caseload initially comprised of 25 children, but in less than a year it grew to 40. These children had developmental delays or disabilities, and I would visit them once a week for an hour of therapy, which I provided in their homes. While working there, I was able to hone a specialized communication skill that reversed communication disorders in children, resulting in full recovery or a reverse diagnosis.

"Once word got around town, many families dropped their current speech therapists (including at the business where I worked), and wanted to get on board with me. I was able to initiate communication in children within two to four hours (completely unheard of), while speech therapists worked with a child for six months to a year, and made incremental or no progress.

"Many of my clients referred me to their friends and relatives; some people relocated to the area just to be seen by me. It was at this time that negative events began occurring.

"It seemed that the more successful and well known I became, the wife (owner) became resentful, intimidated, and insecure, responding to me by being distant, cold, and unwilling to communicate.

"I walked in unexpectedly to hear the owner and other therapists gossiping nastily about my work and me. The owner had no desire to communicate directly with me, and instead manipulated the situation until the office was so dysfunctional it was beyond repair.

"It was not until years after that I realized I worked for a bully, and although it took some time, I did forgive her.

"In retrospect, I learned that the bully had a strong influence over the others, who had never got to know me as a person and professional. The bully knew this, and took advantage."

I asked Julie what she would need in order to trust this person again. This is what she wrote:

"The scars remain, but for her own sake and for making things right, I would want an apology, not just to me, but also in public with the admission of her ulterior motives for her libel and slander."

Lessons from Julie's story

- **Talk to people in your office, and get to know them.** If Julie had done this, staff would have been less likely to believe gossip.

- **Trust your instincts.** If you believe things aren't going well, speak up.

- **Find a mediator you trust.** If you don't feel you can talk to a person, work with someone who can, and will, speak on your behalf.

- **There are always three perspectives:** yours, theirs, and an outside observer's. In the book *Difficult Conversations*, authors Sheila Heen, Bruce Patton, and Douglas Stone show how to look at these conversations as opportunities to learn and grow.

Difficult Conversations

It would be wonderful if we could go through life knowing the perfect thing to say at every moment. The reality is that we all have times when we have difficulty communicating things that are important to us. In fact, sometimes it is the emotion invested in the moment that causes the difficulty.

I've created the following worksheets to help navigate difficult conversations.

Understand What Is Happening

- What is the problem from my point of view?
- What is important to me?
- What is the problem from their point of view?
- What is important to them?
- What has been my contribution to the current difficult situation? What did I do, or not do?
- How could I change my contribution?
- What has been their contribution? What did they do, or not do?

Separate *Impact* from *Intent*!

- What were my intentions?
- What impact did their actions have on me, and how did I react?
- What might have their intentions been?
- What impact might my actions have had on them, and how did they react?

What You Know About *FEELINGS AND EMOTIONS*

- What are my feelings about what happened? (Use the Plutchik diagram below to find the feeling word.)
- Which of my feelings are hard for me to express?
- What feelings might the other person be having? Which feelings might I have trouble recognizing?
- What is my purpose for having this conversation?
- What do I hope to accomplish? (If your purpose is to prove how right you are, then don't bother!)

Plutchik Map of Emotions[4]

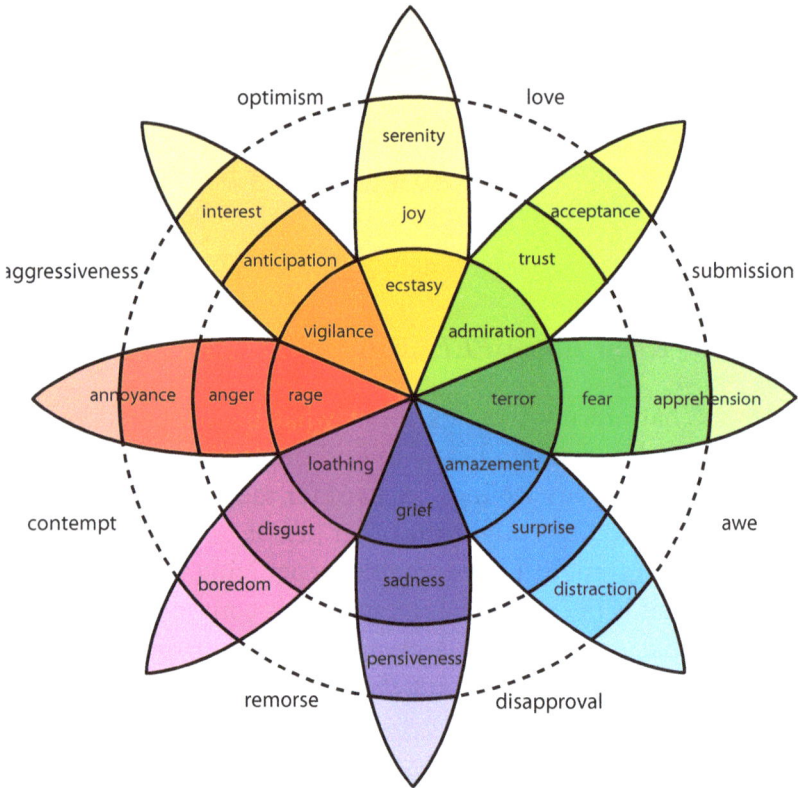

From the stories I've heard, the biggest betrayals were from people that were initially trusted, and in the *inner circle* of trust.

Ingrid's story of her brother's betrayal

"Several years ago my sister passed away, and after her funeral I found out that my brother, whom I had adored, had been stealing from her, as her Power of Attorney, and subsequently also had her will and all her property signed over to him.

---

4 Reprinted with permission

"I know what my sister had wanted, and essentially it was for all her nieces and nephews (she had no children) and our mother to be the recipient of her estate. I had promised I would make sure of that. However, my brother ensured that he got his hands on everything. I was incredibly hurt and shocked for years, and eventually became indifferent toward him. I no longer have a relationship with him.

"More recently, after having come to terms with all of that, I found out he entered my matrimonial home, while my ex and I were going through a bitter divorce, and helped himself to my things. The behavior, as nasty as it was, I could almost understand from my ex, but my own brother? My kids and I had to start all over again from scratch. I had nothing that used to be mine when I left. This was, for me, the worst betrayal of trust ever. Although I am no longer angry, I can never trust him again, nor will I ever have a relationship with him the way I did. I can forgive and move on, but he no longer has meaning in my life in any significant way. I mourned the loss of my brother, and now I am done."

I asked Ingrid if there is anything her brother could do to rebuild the trust. Here is what she said

"I have pondered over that same thing many times over. I think acknowledgement of what he has done to his family would have been a start, but I realized that that would never happen, as he must have somehow felt justified in doing what he did.

"A few years afterward, I got a call from his wife, my sister-in-law, to tell me he was in the hospital facing quadruple bypass surgery, and needed *his family*. I thought how ironic it was that when faced with his own mortality, suddenly he needed us. I never went to see him, but passed on my sentiments. When he fully recovered, we were out of the picture again.

" At this stage, an apology might be a start, but again, the damage was done and my trust is clearly broken. I couldn't say for sure if it could be rebuilt, and if so, it would take a great deal of time and some sort of proof that he earned trust. As cliché as it sounds, I can forgive, but not so sure I can forget, and that memory will always hold me back from ever trusting him.

"I now investigate crimes against seniors, and power of attorney abuse is in the forefront of my investigations. If I had known then what I know now, things would have been different, and he would never have gotten away with it.

"In the end, I would still not have trusted him any more than now. I now have a better understanding of how money, greed and desperation drives people to do things so extraordinary, even at the risk of betraying those closest to them, and justify it all by their own narcissistic drives."

Lessons from Ingrid's story

- Trust, but verify. Involve a neutral third party to monitor accounts.

- The most vulnerable are the most at risk of having their trust broken. Create checks and balances to ensure they are protected.

- Make sure that wishes are in writing.

- Perpetrators are most likely to be an adult, children, or someone close to a person. They may be going through their own financial problems, and be experiencing stress.

Josh's Story of Losing *Business* Trust

Josh Freedman is the CEO of Six Seconds, an organization founded in 1997 to promote and grow emotional intelligence around the globe. They have members in 167 countries and offices, and representatives in 25. Their goal is to have a billion people practicing emotional intelligence.

This is what Josh told me.

"I was coaching a Chief Operational Officer, who had lost trust in a Regional Director who reported to her. What I noticed is that she did not *realize* she'd lost trust in him until it was really bad. For months, she doubted him because he was "too positive" and he seemed to make things sound better than they really were. Meanwhile, he was afraid to be honest because he thought she would overreact. So there was a seed of distrust that grew until there was no real choice but to terminate him. I don't think it was possible to rebuild because the distrust was sort of "in the shadows." Neither of them were willing to own it. By the time it was too evident to ignore, it was too dysfunctional to repair."

Lessons from Josh's story

- Be open and honest in your communication.
- Don't wait until things are bad before you bring something up.
- Check in with your emotions on a regular basis. If something doesn't feel right, explore why.

Josh's Story of Losing Personal Trust

"I felt betrayed by my step-father due to many years of untrustworthy behavior: affairs he had while he was with my mother, lying, and not doing what he said he'd do.

"We had a difficult conversation in which I told him how I felt. There was a time in his life when he was "on the rocks" and he really wanted connection. We didn't set any specifics like, "do this and I'll trust you again," but I told him that it was important that he show up and be present. We made a mutual commitment to build a better relationship, recognizing that while he was the major instigator of the breakdown, the relationship was our shared job.

"I didn't ask him to totally change. For example, I never expected that he'd arrive at our house on the named hour — but I did expect that if he said he'd come at 1:00 pm Saturday, he'd arrive *sometime* Saturday!

"To distill ten years down, we developed a very good relationship. He became a very important part of my life and my kids' lives. It's perhaps strange, but in the end I trusted him with big things: to care, to be open, to listen, and to participate in our lives. I didn't trust him when it came to practicalities and day-to-day details. For example, at Christmas I would meet with him, and we'd shop together to make sure he hadn't forgotten to buy gifts for anyone — and December 24th turned out to be some of the best days."

Lessons from Josh's Story on Losing Personal Trust

- Get to know someone, and expect them to be who they say they are. Tell them what you need, but be realistic in your expectations.

Joscelyn's Story

It is close to 20 years since Joscelyn found out she had Lupus. I can't write the phrase *suffers with Lupus* because nothing is further from how she lives her life.

She is a talented writer who has a monthly column with *Psychology Today,* and is sought after to share her wisdom and talents through speaking and coaching.

Joscelyn has the healthiest lifestyle of all my friends. She eats healthy, exercises on a regular basis, and takes care of her emotional and spiritual health. It's always delightful to be around her, since she exudes health and vitality.

Before this diagnosis she was in her peak of health, running for miles up mountain trails, and living a vibrant and active life. She is so in tune with her body, that when things didn't quite feel right she went to her doctor to head off potential problems.

As empowered as she was in taking care of her own body, she needed external help from doctors. In reaching out for help, three separate specialists all dismissed what she was describing, and prescribed drugs.

Joscelyn knew there was something more; something major; but by the time she was listened to — correction — by the time she found herself in the hospital's trauma ward, it was almost too late.

When you are that sick you trust that the doctors will do all that they can to save your life, including seeking outside counsel. That didn't happen, and these doctors broke trust with Jocelyn. But I'll let her tell her own story:

I do everything in my power to stay healthy, by nurturing my body through diet, daily exercise and plenty of rest. What's difficult is that when anything extreme happens to my body, and it isn't remedied quickly, the shock to my immune system can trigger a life-threatening lupus flare. When the fluid started to build on my abdomen, I spoke to my doctors immediately. When those pleas were ignored, the fluid continued to build – 10 lbs, 15lbs, 25lbs, 50lbs of fluid pushing on my every organ, keeping me from being able to eat.

75

It took countless phone calls and visits from my family members to my specialist's office to have her take action. The fluid was filling my lungs, and could have been deadly. Then things went from bad to worse: when I finally convinced the doctor to do a procedure to remove the fluid, it went horribly wrong, landing me in the trauma ward, with no electrolytes in my body.

With continued shock to my system – E-coli, the stress of the fluid, lack of nourishment, and the draining of nearly all my magnesium – the result was a severe lupus flare that crippled my kidneys and liver.

Long story short, after three months in and out of hospital, being sent home without answers, and pleading to be admitted again when things grew progressively worse, the only thing the lead specialist, who had denied me help for so long, had left to tell me was that I was going to die!

How does one then go on to trust doctors and surgeons? For me, it was about focusing on the doctors who cared and would never let me die. When that specialist told me I was going to die, I went to another doctor, and requested a blood transfusion to be able to fly across the country, where I worked with two specialists I trusted. Within ten minutes (ten minutes!!) one of them determined that I had a blood clot in my abdomen. He was right. All I needed all along were blood thinners, and a lack of compassion from several doctors had quickly twisted this journey from a single remedy, to one of a nearly devastating ending.

I'm alive today because two compassionate specialists flexed their schedules to listen deeply, to what I was experiencing, and provided the care that was needed to help me live another day. (I was hospitalized for a month within one hour of my first appointment with the new specialist.) Compassion meant being willing to ask the necessary questions about what I was experiencing, and read deep into my medical files to solve the root problem.

Lessons from Joscelyn's Story

- Trust isn't earned through a title or a degree. It is earned by how we treat others.

- Above all else, trust yourself. When it comes to you — your body, thoughts, and feelings — you are of foremost authority.

We all have stories. What are your stories of broken trust? What are the lessons you learned from them?

Chapter 4

WHO DO WE TRUST?

Knife Skills

Brandon Chrostowski is a chef, and experienced restaurateur of high-end restaurants around the world. When he launched his French restaurant in Cleveland, Ohio, he decided to staff it with people who had been in prison. Why would he do that?

When he was a young man, he got into trouble, and the judge who saw his case could have sentenced him to ten years in prison. Instead, Brandon was granted leniency and turned his life around. If not for that judge who believed in redemption, his life would have taken a different path. He recognizes himself in each of the people who comes out of jail.

> "Everyone deserves that fair and equal chance."
> - Brandon Chrostowski -

He provides free training, in everything from knife skills, cooking, and the basics of fine wine. The new employees then have the opportunity to use their skills in Brandon's restaurant, *Edwins*.

Something Brandon did was take out the security cameras that came with the property. He starts with the belief that everyone deserves a second chance — actually more than a second chance, since he knows that for some of them, the culture they come from may pull them back.

"It's gonna take forgiveness, not seven times but 77 times."
- Brandon Chrostowski -

Around 100 students graduate from the program every year, and the results have been heartwarming. 95% of the graduates find employment after graduation, some in the best restaurants in the city, and the recidivism rate is less than 2%.

The reciprocity of trust has had a positive impact on the city and the future of hundreds of individuals, thanks to Brandon Chrostowski.

When you watch the movie about his restaurant, *Knife Skills*, you can see that Brandon accepts people where they are at the present moment. He trusts them. More often than not, he is rewarded for that trust, as are the people who are a part of the program.

A Story of Personal Trust

My dad ruined many Friday nights for me without even realizing he was doing it! Before I left the house he'd admonish me with the words "Have fun and be good. I trust you." Boy oh boy, what a buzz kill. It was harder to get into trouble hearing those words echoing in my ears.

My friend Debbie didn't have that problem.

One night, we were going to a movie when we saw her Dad's car following us behind the bus. We tried to ditch him by getting off early and walking an extra few blocks to the theatre, going through areas he couldn't follow. You can imagine how well that played out for her when she got home!

When I got home that night my Dad asked where we had been. When I told him what had happened, that we had been followed, so we got off the bus early and walked to the theatre, he said he already knew. Debbie's father had gone over to my house to tell my father what he had found out on his spying mission.

My Dad told me that he trusted that we had gone to the theatre, but added that if he found out otherwise, I'd be in big trouble. He also told Debbie's dad "to mind his own damn business", because he trusted his kids.

I don't know anyone who had a perfect childhood, and my parents and I made our fair share of mistakes when it came to our trust relationship. Debbie had a much rougher time. Her father tapped into her phone calls, followed her, and scrutinized everything she did.

When she was fifteen, she said to me, "They already believe the worst, so I may as well do it and have fun." Following her own advice resulted in her pregnancy at the age of sixteen.

I know from raising my own kids that it isn't always easy to trust, especially when they are going through their teen years, and testing their limits. Heck, I remember the toddler years when they could lie about not taking a cookie while they were biting into it!

Be realistic. When your child lies — and it's going to happen by the best of kids to the most brilliant parents — relax. If it's a big problem, get help.

Rocky – A Lesson in Trust

My niece was visiting us in Philadelphia, and we did a day of following in the footsteps of the character, Rocky, played by Sylvester Stallone, in his 1976 movie. The movie came out years before she was born, but not only did she know it well, even her children knew of the iconic character. I love the movie too, and every time I see it I learn something new.

We walked through the Italian market, and of course, had to finish our day running the steps at the Philadelphia Museum of Art, pumping our arms in the air at the top of the stairs, just as Rocky did in the movie. I don't think I've ever been to the museum without seeing someone do this.

We ended the day watching the movie, and although I've seen it many times, I still noticed new things about the character. It showed me why the movie still resonates with people more than 40 years after it was made.

His character was able to see the motivation behind the words of others, and showed them through his actions that he could be trusted to keep their secrets, accept their weaknesses, and always see the best in them. What a great way to build trust!

That is why people take the pilgrimage through all of the places Rocky visited, and why he's such a great example of how to build trust!

LEA BROVEDANI

This shows that Sylvester Stallone was able to say so much, even when he said so little. When considering whether I can trust a person or not, I watch what they do and see if aligns with what they say. Rocky didn't say much, but his actions were honorable, and he showed he cared deeply for the people in his life.

Since trust is a feeling, an action, and behavior, it's important that leaders show they care. I'd expect them to be more articulate than Rocky, but he showed emotional intelligence in action, which can be the deciding factor on whether or not we trust.

The Trust Vacation – A Business Story

I have a great friend, who has her phone with her at all times, even during vacations. Her staff calls her many times a day, and I wondered if she really had taken time off. She was surprised when I told her to let them make their own decisions, and that if they had to call her every time a decision was needed, that was a trust issue.

5 Cartoon license through Cartoonstock

Her reply was "No, it's not. I'm just there for my staff." But that's not how it works. In order for them to develop trust in themselves, and for her to show her trust, she has to step away.

If she wants them to develop their skills, then she needs to trust them; by unplugging, and allowing them to make decisions, she will show them that she does.

Are you able to unplug from technology? How many times did you check your emails when you were on vacation to see if there were any problems at work that you felt you needed to answer?

My husband holds a senior position in his company, and we're always looking for holidays where technology can't find us. Our favorite one so far was white water rafting down the Colorado River, in the Grand Canyon.

His staff were told that if there was an emergency, they could contact him by calling the rafting company, which would then make a call on the satellite phone, which was only turned on at specific times at checkpoints along the way. They got the hint that it would have to be a pretty big problem in order for them to justify a call.

He reassured them that he trusted they had the skills and abilities to handle any problem, and he was rewarded with two weeks without technology. His staff was given a strong message that they were trusted. Even though there were a few fires that needed to be put out, his staff stepped up and challenged themselves to solve the issues without running to him. It developed deeper trust among the team, and greater respect for each other.

Risk Taking

Illustration by Phillip Brovedani
The Trust Fall

If we want to strengthen trust, we need to use it — and that means giving people opportunities to go a little further than they did yesterday.

When the (now) COO of Six Seconds, Josh Freedman, first started traveling to develop international offices, it was with the trust and blessing of his mentor and advisor, Anabel Jensen. Anabel knew important decisions would set the course for the global operation of Six Seconds. She let Josh know she trusted him to make decisions in negotiating contracts overseas.

She said, "I know you'll make the right decisions because you're the one who will be there making them!" Josh tells me her faith and support in his abilities gave him the confidence to step into his bigger role of COO.

In my book *TRUSTED — Secret Lessons from an Inspired Leader*, Hunter Birkett (the protagonist) talks with Susan Cannon (his boss and mentor) about the competency levels of his staff. Birkett tries to figure out who he can trust with different projects, and spends time looking at the experience, skills, and abilities of each of his staff. He also wants to determine how much coaching, mentoring, and supervision each of them needs.

(We'll be visiting Hunter a few more times throughout the book since he can show us what not to do, and how you can learn to be more trustworthy.)

He has created a hierarchy of abilities, starting at level one, where someone needs a lot of direction, to level ten, where Hunter can employ a hands-off approach, and let his employee take complete responsibility.

One employee is causing Hunter a lot of concern. Hunter is evaluating him at a lower level, and micro managing him because of mistakes that have been made and assignments that weren't delivered on time. Susan has worked with this employee for years, and tells Hunter that in all the years they've worked together, he was the most reliable and trustworthy person she's had.

She helps Hunter see that his perspective of this employee is one of the reasons for the distrust. "When things don't add up," she tells him, "it's time to do some digging."

In the story, the employee is having difficulty at home that is affecting his work performance, but he doesn't share that with anyone at work. Because of Susan's insights, Hunter has an open and deep conversation with the employee, and trust starts to grow.

Susan tells Hunter he must learn to recognize where to put people on the competency ladder. Put them too high and you'll have employees fail because they can't do the job. Put them too low, and you lose people because they aren't being challenged enough.

85

Susan's advice is to take a step back and assess each employee's competency so that he is not expecting a "1" to do a job that an "8" should do.

Competency and Trust

I learned the following competency levels from Bob Brooks, Adjunct Facilitator at the University of Phoenix:

1. "Wait to be told." "Do exactly what I say." or "Follow these instructions precisely."

2. "Look into this and tell me the situation. I'll decide."

3. "Look into this and tell me the situation. We'll decide together."

4. "Tell me the situation and what help you need from me in assessing and handling it. Then we'll decide."

5. "Give me your analysis of the situation (reasons, options, pros, and cons) and recommendation. I'll let you know whether you can go ahead."

6. "Decide and let me know your decision, but wait for my go-ahead before proceeding."

7. "Decide and let me know your decision, then go ahead unless I say not to."

8. "Decide and take action – let me know what you did (and what happened)."

9. "Decide and take action. You need not check back with me."

10. "Decide where action needs to be taken, and manage the situation accordingly. It's your area of responsibility now."

I know, from experience, that Bob's list makes a huge difference in how to manage staff.

You do your employees a disservice when you put them in positions and then over- supervise them. The reverse is also true. You do a disservice when you expect them to do what they have no skill, ability, or training to do.

What about you?

Where would you place your staff?
Where would you place yourself?
Where would your boss place you?

If you want to develop a trusted workplace, understand the competencies of you and your staff, and then ask yourself, "What do I need to do to help them to move up one level?" It starts with taking a trust vacation — stepping just far enough away from a responsibility so that others can pick up the slack.

Losing the Secure Job

Susan Sweeney is a close friend and a brilliant businesswoman. She was one of the leading experts on internet marketing, a multiple award winning speaker, and is currently dean of elearningu.com, an online university that focuses on topics for the tourism industry.

Earlier in her career, she was working for Industry Canada, when they had a department-wide downsizing. Many of the people who worked for the department were worried about their jobs, and what they would do if they were laid off. Jobs with Industry Canada were secure, paid well, and for many, the only job they had ever had. Even back then, Susan had an entrepreneurial spirit. She wasn't worried, but she could see that many of her colleagues were.

Her boss made sure he kept them informed through regular updates on what the government was saying and doing. They knew he would tell them the truth, and would not hide any bad news from them.

He met with all the staff and told them he knew a lot of them were finding this extremely stressful, but suggested that, quite often, the thought about a situation is more stressful than the situation itself. He asked them to imagine the worst-case scenario and what their reality would be if the worst happened. Then, once they had a grasp on that and what it would be, he told them to imagine what to do.

"You might find it's not as bad as you first imagined," he said. He showed them that even if they were laid off, they would have a healthy severance package and there were other jobs to apply for.

He was able to give them the news, and at the same time, deal with their concerns in a compassionate way that focused on the future. He didn't criticize or downplay what was happening, but showed them how to focus on a positive future.

Even more than 20 years later, when Susan thinks of a boss she trusted, he comes to mind.

The Reciprocity of Trust

If a group member shares information, and other members reciprocate in kind, the team performs better, and it shows in the work they produce.

What happens when each member holds on to critical information, and everyone has to dig around to find the answers to a question? Later it's found out that one member of the team knew all along and didn't share the information! Now imagine asking that team member why they didn't share and being told,

"No one asked me."

As a leader, have your team share their areas of expertise and key information, so others know where to get critical information. We trust others who are willing to share and cooperate.

If you're building a trust culture, be aware that people will repay trust with trust. Smart leaders know this. Picture being told by your boss on the first day of your job, "I've heard great things about you, and completely trust that you'll do an amazing job." How hard will you work to live up to that expectation?!

Compare that to the ground zero trust expectation of, "I don't trust anyone when they start. You'll have to prove you can be trusted."

I've worked for both, and I can tell you that I blossomed with the first boss, and withered with the second.

Trust is like a game of tennis — it can only continue when it goes back and forth between players. In a healthy trust relationship, we trust and are trusted to the same degree.

Keeping Safe from Scams

The wild wild west had nothing on the internet. How many of us have had the same prince from an African country offer to send us millions, if we just gave him our banking information so he could do the wire transfer? There are so many variations that the scam, regardless of where it is from, is called *The Nigerian Letter Scam*.

Here is an example of the letter (my comments are italicized and bolded):

Dear Friend,

As you read this, I don't want you to feel sorry for me because, I believe everyone will die someday. *(It starts with an emotional appeal)*

My name is Peter Lawson, a merchant in Dubai, in the U.A.E. I have been diagnosed with esophageal cancer, which was discovered very late due to my laxity in carrying for my health. It has defiled all forms of medicine, and right now, I have only about a few months to live, according to the medical experts.

I have not particularly lived my life so well, as I never really cared for anyone, not even myself, but my business. Though I am very rich, I was never generous. I was always hostile to people, and only focus on my business; as that was the only thing I cared for. But not now I regret all this, as I now know that there is more to life than just wanting to have or make all the money in the world. I believe when God gives me a second chance to come to this world I would live my life a different way from how I have lived it.

Now that God has called me, I have willed and given most of my properties and assets to my immediate and extended family members and as well as a few close friends. I want God to be merciful to me and accept my soul, and so I have decided to give arms to charity organizations and give succor and confort to the less priviledged *(the letters usually have spelling mistakes)* in our societies, as I want this to be one of the last good deeds I do on earth.

So far, I have distributed money to some charity organizations in the U.A.E., Algeria and Malaysia. Now that my health has deteriorated so badly, I cannot do this my self anymore. I once asked members of my family to close one of my accounts and distribute the money which I have there to charity organization and to the less privledged in Bulgaria and Pakistan, they refused, and kept the money to themselves. Hence, I do not trust them anymore, as they seem not to be contended with what I have left for them.

The last of my money, which no one knows of, is the huge cash deposit of twenty four million dollars, that I have with a Security Company in Europe for safe keeping. I will want you to help me collect this deposit and disburse it to some charity organizations and to the less privledged.

Please send me a mail to indicate if you will assist me in this disbursement.

I have set aside 10% for you, for your time, and patience.

You can email me at:plawson@hknetmail.com

While I await to hear from you, may God be with you and your entire family.

Remain blessed,

Mr. Peter Lawson

It astounds me that anyone would fall for this, but for the scammers it's a numbers game. If you send out a million letters and get a .05% success rate, you're making money. Those who are willing to assist are asked to provide their bank account number for "safekeeping" the funds, and very detailed personal information. Sometimes they are asked to send money to the letter sender for taxes and various fees. The victims never see their money again, and the con artist now has the ability to steal their identity and wipe out their bank accounts.

I've received a variation of this with someone posing as a colleague I highly respect, saying she was in Europe, and embarrassed to let anyone know she had run out of funds. The letter asked me to send her money through Western Union, and not embarrass her.

I've heard of elderly people being conned this way, by someone posing as their grandchild. It's despicable. One of the latest is a call purporting to be from the Canada Revenue Agency, telling you that you are in arrears, asking for all your contact information, and demanding that you send a bank transfer. My friend Helen said she had a call from someone with a deep Southern accent saying that they were from the CRA — that gave us both a chuckle!

Here is what you can do to protect yourself against online scammers:

- If you receive a letter from Nigeria, or any other country, asking you to send personal or banking information, do not reply! Just delete!

- If you receive an appeal from a family member or friend, don't send anything until you have talked to them.

- If you have already responded to such a plea, or if you know someone who is corresponding in this scheme, contact the authorities. There is a fraud division in both the United States and Canada to deal with this.

- Don't fall for strangers offering to place unexpected, large amounts of money at your disposal in exchange for your bank account number or other personal or financial information.

- Cashier checks and money orders can be counterfeit. When a stranger sends a check or money offer to purchase a product or service from you, consult with your bank about the time it will take to verify the check, and wait for the funds to clear.

Who Can We Trust?

We tend to trust people to the extent that they trust us. The diagram below represents a trust circle. I invite you to do two circles; one for the people in your business life, and one for those in your personal life. Where would you place them?

A simple exercise around whom to trust

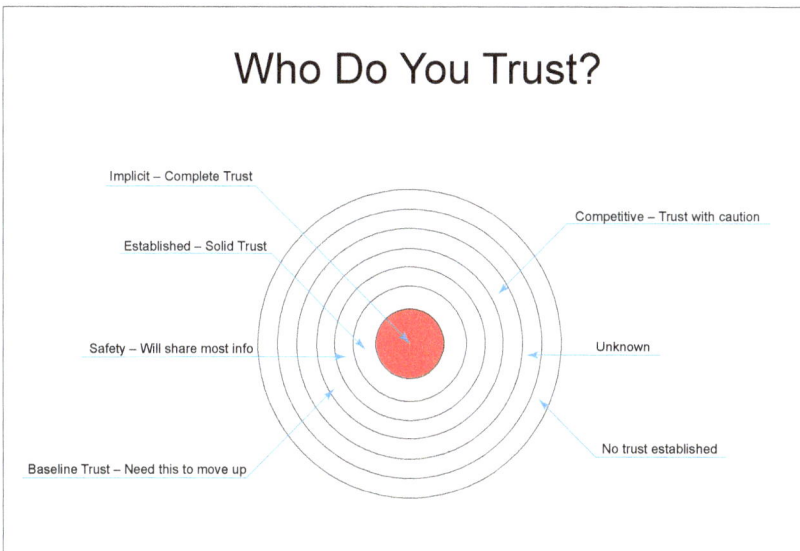

Who Do You Trust?

Implicit – Complete Trust

Competitive – Trust with caution

Established – Solid Trust

Safety – Will share most info

Unknown

No trust established

Baseline Trust – Need this to move up

Reflect on where you put the different people. What are some of the common characteristics of those near the center? How are they generally different from people near the outside? How do the five tenets of trust play out? Remember, they are:

- Caring
- Commitment
- Consistency
- Competence
- Communication

Trust Game

At Northwestern Kellogg, three researchers came up with a game that tested the reciprocity of trust. It was a simple game, where two strangers interacted either face-to-face or anonymously. They weren't told it was a trust game, but rather a game that they could make money just by playing.

The first player received a gift of money; let's say $10.

Now they have a decision to make about player two. They can give that person any amount they like, from nothing to the full $10. They are told that whatever they decide to send is going to be tripled on its way to the second player, so if they send the whole $10 the second player gets $30.

The second player then has a choice to return as much, or as little, as they want to the first player.

Why would player one trust? Why would player two reciprocate?

What they found was that the more the first player trusts and risks, the more the second player trusts and reciprocates.

If you have a deficit of trust, it's time to look inside and see if you have behaviors that create distrust. As the researchers found at Northwestern Kellogg, how much we trust has a major impact on how much we're trusted.

You can use your trust circles as a guide. What brings people toward the center? Are you doing the same kind of behaviors and commitments?

You have to be able to see the big picture, rather than the immediate payback.

Like many people, when I distrust someone I want to close down, and stop talking to them. I make assumptions that are rarely good. Then, I may call my best friend and talk it out with her. She has an outside observer opinion, and is willing to tell me another way to look at the situation, helping me formulate the conversation she knows I'd want to have with them.

I take out my "Difficult Conversation" worksheets from Chapter 3, and fill them out, which makes it easier when I sit across from the person and talk it through. Broken trust is often the result of miscommunication and misunderstanding, and like you, I need all the help I can get.

If I discover what the person did was intentionally deceiving, it tells me a lot about the person, and I know where to place them in my trust circle.

When there's a serious trust breach in business, relationships are damaged — sometimes irreparably. You might work with the person who has broken trust; you might cooperate with them; you might have a beneficial relationship. But you are unlikely to really trust them.

In your business relationships, think about the money you'll save by keeping those trust relationships healthy. Take the time to have the conversations before trust is damaged permanently.

Chapter 5

LEADERSHIP, PURPOSE AND TRUST

According to an article in the *Harvard Business Review*, roughly half of all managers don't trust their leaders. In a survey done at the University of Chicago, four out of five had "only some" or "hardly any" confidence in the people running major corporations. It sounds as if leaders seriously need to understand how trust works, and how to rebuild it.

Two competencies are of utmost importance for trusted managers. They are:

1. Inspires and motivates others
2. Displays high integrity and honesty

When I was doing research on trust, I discovered that people see themselves as trusted even when they are not. In a Six Seconds survey of 200 people about trust, leaders generally gave a very different assessment of their own trustworthiness than their employees did.

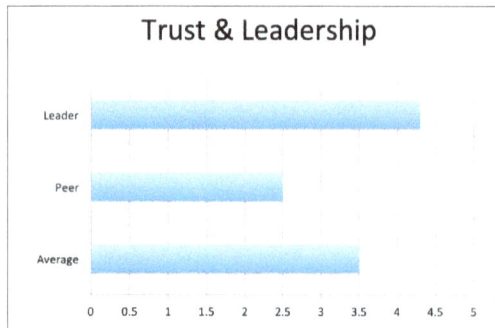

Trust & Leadership

As you can see, leaders gave themselves a score of better than four out of five on trustworthiness. Their peers scored them at less than three.

This discrepancy may be tied to comfortable self-delusion. In my workshops, I've found it easy to get examples from participants of other people breaking trust, but few are willing to share stories of when *they* broke trust. Fortunately, we have the ability to improve, and it starts with admitting that we aren't perfect.

"We are all mistaken sometimes; sometimes we do wrong things, things that have bad consequences. But it does not mean we are evil, or that we cannot be trusted ever, afterwards"

- Alison Croggon –
Australian writer and critic

It is true, none of us are perfect — and frankly, who wants to be?

We may sometimes be overtired, and make an assumption that is not true. When that happens we have to 'fess up and admit we were wrong. But who wants to do that?

Most people associate an admission of guilt with weakness. Let's go back for a moment to my book *TRUSTED - A Leader's Lesson*. Hunter admits to his boss that he is afraid of appearing weak if he apologizes. Susan answers "Hunter, the strength of a leader is measured in the amount of trust others have placed in them."

Think of someone you respect and admire. Is it because they are never wrong? Perhaps it is because they are confident enough to admit their mistakes.

John Caparella, award winning manager and former president of the Venetian resort, one of the top resorts in Las Vegas, Nevada, spoke with Charles Wolfe on PRX radio on how to build trust. He said that when he was opening a new hotel, he challenged his HR team to use this one abiding rule in every decision they made: "Do the right thing."

He modeled the behavior he wanted from others by willingly admitting his own mistakes, and he let staff know they were better served by self-disclosure than not. Most organizations punish a person for making mistakes, which encourages deception. By creating an environment where it was safe to learn from mistakes, Caparella built a team in which open communication, honesty, integrity, and courage were internalized values.

In order for an organization and its leaders to be seen as trustworthy and trusted, leaders should ask themselves two questions as they make decisions and take actions:

1. Is this the action of a trustworthy person?
2. Would I want to read about this in the newspaper?

The Skill of Trust

It's easy to trust when everything is going well, but sometimes there are bumps in the road. The following roadmap will help. I know some of these might seem obvious, but my observation is the obvious isn't always done. Do you see any of these scenarios playing out in your workplace? What would you add?

The Concern	Possible Feelings	Leader Behavior that Builds Trust
Safety Issue eg. Natural disaster or accidents	Fear Worry Unheard	Spend more time explaining options during stressful times. Provide comfort Offer a safety net if possible Be flexible and recognize the job may not be the priority
Changes at work eg. Company is being bought out, merged, or downsizing	Insecurity Doubt Worry Anxiety Anger	Tell them as much as you can as often as you can — even if there is nothing new to add — and make sure your communication is consistent Give reassurance when possible, but don't give false hope
Power struggle eg. employee doesn't get promotion *Or* between managers *Or* between departments	Feeling overlooked and unheard Anger Helplessness Frustration	Provide choices. Listen Address concerns. Define issue problems – does this person believe they should get the promotion because of entitlement (eg. I've been here for x years), or because of work they have done. Tell them why they didn't get the promotion. Tell them what they need to do. Give them goals to work towards.
Lack of teamwork (eg. people are not sharing information. In-fighting. Gossip)	Indifference Checked out Anger	Use "we" more than "I". Emphasize what you have in common. Show shared goals and how meeting them benefits everyone. Share information. Find wins for employees. Get people communicating
What I do doesn't matter.	Anger Resentment Indifference Checked out Frustration Apathy	Demonstrate genuine concern for employees by talking to them, finding out what their concerns are, and having heart-to-heart conversations. Give praise and acknowledgement when they do something right. Communicate to them how their work contributes to business goals
Loss of respect for leadership	Disbelief Distrust Disengagement	Leaders must be able to demonstrate their skills in relation to tasks at hand. Delegate tasks to those who have the experience and competence.
Lack of communication	Hesitation Skepticism Indifference Anxiety	Increase frequency and candor of your communications. Only agree to what you can fulfill. If you can't fulfill a promise, explain why. Cultivate bonds beyond workplace roles when appropriate (eg. team activities that create synergy and camaraderie).

In Dan Ariely's book *The (Honest) Truth about Dishonesty*, he says he has discovered one overriding truth: "We are all dishonest — the difference is in the degree."

If we see dishonesty as a continuum from one to ten, with one being totally dishonest, and ten being sainthood, most of us lie somewhere in the middle.

1_____10

Are you shaking your head and disagreeing? Are you even saying out loud "Lea, honesty is one of my key values. I am above reproach."

I agree wholeheartedly with Dan Ariely, and it's another reason I don't have truth telling as part of my trust model.

People lie for many different reasons. Sometimes they lie to protect the ego of the other person. "Honey, does this outfit make me look fat?" We tell the lie to preserve our relationships.

How about the lies we tell ourselves? Everything from "I can't lose weight because I have a slow metabolism" to "I wish I could (fill in the blank), but I don't have the time, money, skill, or something else".

At the center of trust, is our trust in ourselves, and that starts with keeping promises to ourselves, not lying to ourselves, and expecting more of ourselves than we do of others.

Business Trust

I'm glad Google dropped "Don't be Evil" as the first statement in its code of conduct in early 2018. I always wondered how that could be used to drive them to trustworthy behavior.

Although it is still mentioned, it has now been relegated to the end, and the code is now based on what they want, and not on what they don't want.

The Google Code of Conduct

"The Google Code of Conduct is one of the ways we put Google's values into practice. It's built around the recognition that everything we do in connection with our work at Google will be, and should be, measured against the highest possible standards of ethical business conduct.

We set the bar that high for practice as well as aspirational reasons: Our commitment to the highest standards helps us hire great people, build great products, and attract loyal users. Respect for our users, for the opportunity, and for each other are foundation to our success, and are something we need to support every day.

And remember... don't be evil, and if you see something that you think isn't right — speak up."

Greed vs Purpose

When my children were learning to talk, one of the first words they said was *why*. They wanted to know the reasons for doing things, for figuring out their world, and I quickly found out that trying to give them a non-answer just resulted in more *whys*.

As adults we still want to know *why*, and it turns out the noble *why* we do things has a greater impact on profitability than the financial *why*.

Research organization, EY Business, researches how purpose drives business success. They show how the *why*, or the purpose for which we do things, has more to do with our success than being financially driven.

In their survey of 474 business executives around the world, 90% agreed that having a purpose drove performance and profits, but only 46% said it informed their decision making.

That is profound! Think about how you and your company frame your decisions to your team. What a difference it could make to your team if you showed them the purpose.

In the survey, EY Business defined organizational purpose as "an aspirational reason for being, which inspires and provides a call to action for an organization, its partners, and stakeholders, and provides benefit to local and global society."

Building a Cathedral

A traveller came upon three bricklayers. He asked the first man what he was doing, and the man answered that he was laying bricks. He asked the second man the same question, and the man answered he was putting up a wall. When he asked the third man the same question, he said he was building a cathedral.

They were all doing the same thing, but the first man had a job, the second man had a career, and the third man had his purpose.

Who would you trust to do the best work? Who does the work in your organization — bricklayers or cathedral builders?

When you are looking to inspire and motivate others, can you show them how their position aligns with the purpose of the organization?

Chapter 6

ETHICS – TRUST IN ACTION

Merriam-Webster Dictionary defines ethics this way:

Ethics
Ethics/
noun
the discipline dealing with what is good and bad, and
with moral duty and obligation.

Leaders who are known for their strong ethics succeeding in
business, but it sometimes feels that looking for leaders with
strong ethics is much like the ancient Greek philosopher
Diogenes with his lantern, looking for an honest man without
ever finding one. Perhaps that's because stories of corruption
and dishonesty are more titillating than stories of ethical leaders
doing the right thing.

You'll see a vision and mission statement in most company
offices, but do they follow them? Ethics involves staying true to
your beliefs, even when it is difficult.

What if the belief is winning at all costs, and the person stays
true to that belief. Is that person ethical?

No! Ethics involves morality *and* goodness.

When I was writing *TRUSTED* I wanted to show that Hunter, the protagonist, was flawed but ethical. Even though he really messed up and ran the business into the ground, he met with each of his employees personally to tell them of the demise of the company. Then he sat and faced their anger and told them the truth, even though it was uncomfortable.

That was based on an experience I witnessed when my husband was working for a company on an expat assignment in India. The contract was supposed to last for three years, but within six months of living in India, my husband and his colleagues realized that the client company was going to be breaking the contract.

For four months they had been putting in 12 – 16 hour days, six days a week. Birthdays were missed and relationships suffered, but the spoken and unspoken message was that the experience gained on this complex international project would be a boon to their careers. Then rumors started surfacing that there were going to be layoffs. A few weeks later they were stunned when the boss flew in from the U.S. head office and brought the team together. He said, "We're going to re-interview all of you since we aren't sure we have the right people on the job. If we find you aren't right for this position, we'll find something else for you."

The next day, he flew back to head office and left the interviews to an HR team. He wasn't available for any questions or support, and his absence was viewed as uncaring and self-serving. If there were pressing reasons for his disappearance, he didn't communicate them during the meeting he held with them.

Some knew that the leaders in the company in India had faced him with a difficult decision and he had been backed into a corner. The interviews were at the Indian company's insistence, but his team judged him by the impact of the deed, how it was communicated, and his actions immediately afterwards. Like many leaders, he probably didn't see this as an ethical lapse, but ethical leaders protect and stand up for their team.

Trust is directly impacted by ethics. What were his ethical obligations?

Ethics involve the Golden Rule, "Do unto others as you would have them do unto you." Would he have been okay if this was done to him?

Ethics impacts trust levels. Ethics means going beyond legality and asking, "Is it right and just?"

When he left the team in India, and in the absence of information, people filled in the void, and true to human nature, they believed the worst. After the interviews, a number of people were let go and told to find another position within the company. Trust within the division was at an all time low.

Douglas R. May, Professor and Co-Director of the International Center for Ethics in Business said the nine steps to ethical decision-making developed by Linda Trevino and Katherine Nelson are the gold standard for ethics in business.

1. Gather the facts.
1. Define the ethical issues.
2. Identify the affected parties (stakeholders).
3. Identify the consequences.
4. Identify the obligations (principles, rights, justice).
5. Consider your character and integrity.
6. Think creatively about potential actions.
7. Check your gut.
8. Decide on the proper ethical action, and be prepared to deal with opposing arguments.

This situation could have been very different if the boss had applied these nine steps when he was meeting with his team.

Using the *Five Tenets of Trust* would have also helped him to arrive at an ethical and just solution.

1) **Commitment:** The boss made a commitment to help the staff that was laid off. Resources should have been made available instead of letting everyone flounder. If he couldn't keep the commitment he should have let people know why.

2) **Caring:** What a difference it would have made for his reputation if he had scheduled time to talk to each of the employees who were laid off. Flying in and out as soon as he gave the bad news was seen as cold and uncaring.

3) **Consistency:** What was said and what was done didn't jibe.

4) **Competence:** People will question your competence if they don't see it in action. He didn't communicate his reasons for decisions that affected his staff's livelihood, and he was the person who had put them in their positions.

5) **Communication:** The other four competencies are based on a solid foundation of communication.

In face to face communication, much of what is communicated is the feelings behind the words. When you are having a conversation with someone, do they have your full attention? Are you making eye contact? Are you allowing the frustrations of the day to affect the tone of your voice? If one of your staff comes into your office with something important to say, close your computer, come from behind the desk, and give them your full attention. It's one of the many small things you can do to build trust.

The recipe for trust building is to make small agreements, keep them, and then make larger commitments, and keep them. Clarify expectations, since unclear expectations can undermine communication and trust. Always communicate immediately if you cannot keep a promise, and clean up broken commitments immediately. As a leader you will make promises that others need to carry out for you. Follow up to make sure your promises have been kept. You will be judged by how well you follow up, and your character will be judged on how well you accept responsibility.

I learned the last part about delegation the hard way, when I first started managing people. When I promised to get something done, I would often pass on the task, and then forget about it. There were times when the delegated tasks weren't done, and of course my staff were disappointed in me for not doing what I said would be done. I learned always to check to make sure my promises were kept, even when they were supposed to have been carried out by someone else.

Rulebook on Ethical Leadership

Ethical leaders think long term. They set high moral standards, and act in accordance with them. They understand behaviors that are good and right, and they can be transparent because they have nothing to hide. They are consistent in what they tell others to do, and how they conduct themselves. The more they *walk the talk,* by translating the values they espouse and what they do, the more they are trusted and respected by others.

It can seem daunting, since it's rare that all decisions are black and white, and ethical dilemmas happen when neither choice gives you a perfect outcome. When making the decision, try asking yourself, "Which decision would I want to read about in the newspaper?"

Ethical decision making also involves a process of inquiry; asking questions about what is right and what is wrong.

Two top leadership gurus, Jim Kouzes and Barry Posner, started working together over thirty years ago. Their model is still the gold standard for ethical leaders. If you're looking for a process to follow, their The Five Practices of Exemplary Leadership® is a great place to start. Here are the five practices, followed by my own take.

1. Model the Way

   This is an important practice because it is how leaders earn, sustain, and build trust. In my *Five Tenets of Trust*, this would show up as consistency.

2. Inspire a Shared Vision

   When leaders can inspire their teams to commit to a shared goal, they create a strong force that sustains the energy and focus to achieve.

3. Challenge the Process

   Leaders who commit to a goal realize they must change, grow, and adapt to continually produce solid results over time. Process is about finding new and better ways of doing things.

4. Enable Others to Act

   At the heart of every great team is strong trust. A climate where people know they can share ideas without ridicule or scorn, can make a mistake, use it as a learning opportunity, and feel personal power and ownership, is a winning combination that creates success. It starts with enabling others.

5. Encourage the Heart

   Caring is the first of my *Five Tenets of Trust,* and with good reason. Part of a leader's job is to let people know they are more than a cog in the wheel. Care shows up as encouragement and simple actions. Celebrating hard work and achievements, personal thanks, and encouragement when it is needed are all ways of showing you care as a leader, and encourage the heart.

The Dastardly – why the untrustworthy never win in the end

What do Madoff, Skilling, Volkswagen, and United Airlines have in common? If you answered they all demonstrated unethical behavior, you'd be correct.

Bernie Madoff was sentenced, in 2008, to 150 years in prison. He will die behind bars for his crime, since time off for good behavior will never add up to enough years to let him see freedom. He persuaded people to trust him with their money, promising high returns by relying on new investors to supply the cash. It was a Ponzi scheme and was named after 1930s swindler Charles Ponzi who conned investors into giving him millions of dollars, and paid them returns with other investors' money.

Madoff cheated investors out of more than 65 billion dollars. Many elderly investors lost everything they had, believing him when he said he would take care of them. If you had met Madoff you might have believed in him too. He looked like someone's favorite grandfather, and knew how to speak with soothing tones and reassuring words. He destroyed many lives by his lack of ethics.

Jeffrey Skilling was the head of Enron, which in 2002 was the fifth-largest company in the USA. He and other executives pocketed millions of dollars from illegal gains. When Enron collapsed, billions of dollars in retirement savings and the jobs of thousands of employees vanished. He was said to have an ego that blocked out the sun. His arrogance costed him though, as he served the longest prison term of any executives charged at Enron.

In 2014 **Volkswagen** damaged its impeccable reputation by installing cheating software to fool emission testing on their diesel cars. At the helm of the company were autocratic leaders who bragged about terrifying their staff into achieving at any cost. Each employee was well versed in the 25-page code of conduct, but that was overlooked with the pressure to succeed. When people are afraid, fear trumps ethical behavior as it did at Volkswagen.

When investigating the Volkswagen scandal, Darden professor, Luann Lynch said three deadly factors work together to create a "fraud triangle". It's a perfect recipe for untrustworthy and unethical behavior.

They are:

1. **Pressure** — When pressure from the top is unrelenting, employees can perceive it as succeeding at any cost.

2. **Opportunity** — If cheating makes it easy to succeed, and detecting the cheating is difficult, you provide an opportunity many will seize if they are being pressured.

3. **Rationalization** — In the case of Volkswagen, the engineers rationalized that it was in the best interests of the company. Disgraced CEOs often rationalize that fudging the numbers, lying, or cheating ensures that the company protects employee jobs or stockholder profits by staying profitable.

When the three are all working together, you have a situation where some employees engage in unethical behavior.

I've already told u a few stories about United Airlines, but those stories pale in comparison to the tale of the passenger who was dragged off the United Airlines plane by two security guards. There are pictures of Dr. David Dao being dragged down the aisle of the plane, suffering injuries as they manhandled him. The public was outraged.

The CEO of United gave a weak statement that wouldn't qualify as an apology stating, "This is an upsetting event to all of us here at United." An apology would have followed the SINCERE guidelines that are set out in Chapter 7:

S   Be sorry
I   Intentional
N   No excuses
C   Consequences
E   Empathy
R   Restitution
E   Expect that they may need time.

United took no responsibility for their actions, and did not show how it would change their policies going forward. Do you really trust that they have their customer's best interest at heart?

Learning and Growing into Ethics

I'm proud to be part of *Trust Across America* (TAA). Whenever possible, I like to promote what they do. A few years ago, TAA assembled quotes submitted by their Trust Alliance Members into a poster of weekly dos and don'ts to foster personal and organizational trust. As a member, and past recipient of the *Top Thought Leaders in Trust* award, I wanted to pass on the great tips to my audience.

Every week I Tweeted one of the tips from the poster. At that time, there was a smaller cap on the number of characters you could tweet. If there was room I attributed the quote to the author, but not always.

I was shocked and dismayed when I received an email from Barbara Brooks Kimmel, from *Trust Across America*, telling me she was concerned about at my lack of ethics in retweeting the tips. My intentions were honorable, but the impact created distrust.

I've already given you this quote from Dr. Anabel Jensen, but it's worth repeating:

We judge ourselves by our intentions, and others by their behavior.

As soon as I composed myself, I gave her a call. We discussed why she felt the way she did, and I had a forehead slapping moment when I understood. It looked as if I was publishing the quotes as my own! That was not my intention, but the impact wasn't the positive outcome I had planned.

That incident taught me to ask permission before I publish something if it isn't mine. I know It seems like such an obvious thing now, but I was so intent on getting the messages out about how to increase trust that I didn't consider what I was doing was plagiarism. Seems ironic. Fortunately, Barbara and I cleared up the misunderstanding, and have restored our trusting relationship. She said she didn't see it as an ethics issue, but rather a mistake that was corrected.

I wonder if she trusted my ethics before the phone call. When I spoke with Barbara she said that she believes trust is built over time and in incremental steps and I believe that taking ownership of my mistake and correcting it has helped our relationship.

Plagiarism is a problem and if you want to be trusted, give credit to the originators of any material you use!

We all make mistakes, but if you think your questionable behavior is okay as long as you don't get caught, or your first instinct is to lie when you are confronted, that speaks to your lack of ethics.

My mistake wasn't an ethical breach. It was a mistake I made and then corrected, that would barely register a one on the ethics scale. A real ethical breach is one where the mistake is hidden and compounded.

Integrity and trust are essential for ethical leadership. When leaders have both everyone around can relax, enjoy, and bring their best to what they do.

Integrity follows a moral and ethical code, while trust is your ability to be vulnerable, open, and honest based on positive expectations. You can see that our unethical leaders did not follow a moral or ethical code, and certainly were not open and honest.

The Ethical Leaders

Who do you think of when you think of an ethical person? I think of Nelson Mandela, Melinda Gates, and Mr. Rogers. Each of them has or had a reputation built on integrity and trust. They each realized relationships flourish in a rich environment of trust, respect, integrity, honesty, and compassion.

Nelson Mandela

At different times during his life, Nelson Mandela was branded a convict, an international terrorist, a subversive, and finally as the savior of South Africa. His constant belief in having a country built on the principles of inclusion and equality, in spite of the hardships he went through, was what sustained him during his 27 years in prison.

"I was called a terrorist yesterday, but when I came out of jail, many people embraced me, including my enemies, and that is what I normally tell other people who say those who are struggling for liberation in their country are terrorists. I tell them that I was also a terrorist yesterday, but, today, I am admired by the very people who said I was one." — Nelson Mandela

Mandela was the son of a local chief, and could have lived a life of relative comfort and security, working his job in civil service. He was not groomed to lead, but rather work as counsel for the leader of his tribe. After he became a lawyer, he represented people who were charged with apartheid-related crimes like riding a "whites only" bus, or not carrying proper identification.

He could have left prison earlier if he had agreed to abandon his work for racial equality, but his integrity wouldn't allow it.

He wasn't afraid to trust people with the hard truths, believing that when given the choice they would do the right thing.

When I was in South Africa, I learned the term *Ubuntu*, which is a concept Mandela embraced. He taught that, in the profound sense, we are human only through and because of the humanity of others; that if we are to accomplish anything in this world, it will be in equal measure, due to the work and achievement of others.

Melinda Gates

As one of the richest people in the world, Melinda Gates could have done anything — or nothing.

She chose to use her wealth and power to do good around the world, and focus on helping young women.

She didn't want the limelight, but she knew that if she was going to make a difference in the world, she would have to be willing to put her face and voice to use. Gates believes, in her heart and soul, that giving young girls and women an opportunity to have birth control and family planning improves their lives, and the lives of their children. In countries around the world, access to birth control and family planning has shown to improve not just the lives of women, but the whole family.

After giving a TedX Talk in Germany on family planning and birth control, she was criticized by the Vatican. It was a difficult time for her, as a practicing Catholic, but she continued with her work because of her own strong moral compass and ethics, and seeing the difference her work was making to young women around the world.

She has seen, first hand, the difference she makes. Her belief in helping women from cradle to motherhood shows up in the number of young women who can go to school, how new mothers get prenatal care, and how opportunities are given to start their own businesses.

Mr. Rogers

I loved Mr. Rogers, a North American TV personality, who hosted a children's show called *Mr. Rogers' Neighborhood*. I think everyone who had the chance to watch the show loved him. Every website about him, every comment I could find, said the same thing. He really was as nice in person as he appeared on his show. He was an ordained minister, but after seeing a television show where people were throwing pies at each other, he felt called to produce a show for children that showed better values.

As his stardom rose, media people sent out to interview him, which was difficult because he was so interested in other people that he would be the one asking all the questions. At the end of the interview, they would realize they had spent most of the time talking about themselves!

On one occasion, a limo driver drove him to a meeting. When Mr. Rogers found out the limo driver would have to wait in the car for the two hours while he was in the meeting, he insisted he come in and be included.

On his way home after the meeting, he sat in the front seat with the driver. When the driver casually mentioned they were driving by his house, Mr. Rogers insisted they stop in for a visit with his family. He had supper with them, and entertained everyone by playing the piano.

His values were around respect and recognizing the dignity and potential of all children, and the powerful impact adults have in their lives. He taught through word and deed about being an authentic person of substance.

He believed that helping children navigate their emotions helped them to understand the world around them. He knew that teaching and showing empathy brings understanding and compassion to children, and promotes healthy emotional development. He lived everything he taught. He showed them that they could be loved for being exactly who they were. Mr. Rogers believed in love, compassion, and understanding, and never veered from those values and principles.

Chapter 7

RESTORING TRUST

Johnson & Johnson – An Example of What To do

When James Burke took over as the president of Johnson & Johnson, he asked his managers to review the corporate credo. He was so adamant that they live the credo that he threatened to tear it off the wall if people were not willing to follow it.

Johnson & Johnson Credo:

We believe our first responsibility is to the patients, doctors and nurses, to mothers and fathers, and all others who use our products and services. In meeting their needs, everything we do must be of high quality. We must constantly strive to provide value, reduce our costs, and maintain reasonable prices. Customers' orders must be serviced promptly and accurately. Our business partners must have an opportunity to make a fair profit.

We are responsible to our employees who work with us throughout the world. We must provide an inclusive work environment where each person must be considered as an individual. We must respect their diversity and dignity and recognize their merit. They must have a sense of security, fulfillment, and purpose in their jobs. Compensation must be fair and adequate, and working conditions clean, orderly and safe. We must support the health and well-being of our employees, and help them fulfill their family and other personal responsibilities. Employees must feel free to make suggestions and complaints. There must be equal opportunity for employment, development, and advancement for those qualified. We must provide highly capable leaders, and their actions must be just and ethical.

We are responsible to the communities in which we live and work, and to the world community as well. We must help people be healthier, by supporting better access and care in more places around the world. We must be good citizens — support good works and charities, better health and education, and bear our fair share of taxes. We must maintain in good order the property we are privileged to use, protecting the environment and natural resources.

Our final responsibility is to our stockholders. Business must make a sound profit. We must experiment with new ideas. Research must be carried on, innovative programs developed, investments made for the future, and mistakes paid for. New equipment must be purchased, new facilities provided, and new products launched. Reserves must be created to provide for adverse times. When we operate according to these principles, the stockholders should realize a fair return.

In 1982, seven people died from poisoned Tylenol in the Chicago area. For reasons that have never been discovered, bottles of the medicine were tampered with, and the capsules were replaced with cyanide. People died an agonizing death, and the news media across the nation wrote in detail about the *Tylenol deaths*.

Before the crisis, Tylenol was the most successful over-the-counter pain medication in the world, accounting for 19% of the company's total profits.

Suddenly, the public's trust in Tylenol and Johnson & Johnson was gone.

The FBI tested all the poisoned Tylenol, and found that it came from different manufacturing plants across the United

States. Although all the deaths were in the Chicago area, they determined it didn't originate at the manufacturing plant in Illinois.

Burke was told that as a safety precaution, they should remove the Tylenol in the area. Against the advice of the FBI, the FDA, and many of the people on his board, Burke had all of the Tylenol removed from the shelves throughout North America, and destroyed all the bottles. He put together a task force that created a patented tamper-proof bottle for the pills. The initiative of removing all of the Tylenol, creating the new bottles, and compensating all those affected ended up costing Johnson & Johnson over 100 million dollars.

The way Johnson & Johnson conducted itself during the crisis is still considered one of the best examples of trust in action, and it was because of James Burke's leadership.

Burke received the Presidential Medal of Freedom in 2000, and was named one of the top ten CEOs in the world by *Fortune Magazine* in 2003.

Here is what Burke said about trust in an interview with a leadership magazine:

> "Trust has been an operative word in my life. [It] embodies almost everything you can strive for that will help you to succeed. You tell me any human relationship that works without trust, whether it is a marriage, or a friendship, or a social interaction; in the long run, the same thing is true about business."

Although Burke didn't take credit for the success in handling the crisis at the time, his people said it was his leadership and the belief that he was serious and committed to following the credo that allowed them to make the decisions they did.

When should you apologize?

It depends.

Sometimes it's easy to figure out when to apologize. If you spill red wine on your friend's white carpet...OMG, apologize immediately and profusely. Then get out the stain remover.

You are found cheating, or someone cheats you? You should be apologizing, or you should be accepting an apology. Whether it is cheating in a relationship, or someone is taking credit for somebody else's work, cheating, and lying about it are serious transgressions, and it takes attention, thought, and time to correct them.

Aaron Lazare, author of *On Apology*, suggests you delay your sincere apology until the other party has had an opportunity to process their feelings. A quick "I'm sorry" as soon as the offence has been found out doesn't allow the other person's feelings to surface. They may want to learn more about the situation, and an apology given too soon can appear insincere.

In a business situation, companies have been sidelined because they apologized too late, but too many apologies can also undermine a company's standing in their community. If your company is constantly having to apologize, you've got problems that need to be fixed. So yes apologize, but for goodness sake, go fix the problems!

How to Apologize

The first step is to take responsibility for the action. People want to see ownership of the mistake. Those who are receiving the apology want to believe there is true regret or remorse.

The words "I'm sorry" are magic by themselves. Don't negate the apology by adding "but."

When you apologize, *just* say you are sorry. Don't add excuses, and don't tell the other person they were wrong too. Take the time to find out how the other person is feeling. Don't expect absolution. That is not the purpose of the apology, but hopefully healing will be an outcome.

Acknowledge the consequences of your actions. You wouldn't need to apologize if there wasn't an unwanted consequence.

Give a **SINCERE** apology.

S   Be sorry – be authentic and contrite.
I   Intentional – apologize to all those you affected
N   No excuses – avoid *"if"*, *"but"*, and *"maybe"*
C   Consequences – accept the consequences your actions or words caused
E   Empathy – see it through their eyes
R   Restitution – what will you do going forward?
E   Expect that they may need time.

Ask for forgiveness, but don't get angry if you don't get it right away. Let it go.

Sometimes fast forgiveness can be as insincere as a fast apology.

A SINCERE apology includes both words and actions. It also shows that the wronged person's feelings are important, and the perpetrator is making a commitment to change their behavior going forward. It is giving space to the afflicted, and allowing time for them to heal.

A SINCERE apology requires both parties to care about each other, be courageous, and above all be willing to forgive the other and themselves.

A Dog's Life – Some Companies Never Learn

Dave Carrol's experience with United Airlines happened in 2009. Three years later, I had my own experience with United. Fortunately the outcome wasn't dire, but it was disappointing.

After living in India from 2011 to 2012, we moved to Philadelphia. It was time to reclaim our dog, Booker, who was living with our son, Phill, in Calgary.

Out of all the dogs I've had, Booker is the most goofy, and easy-going. On our walks, tiny children launch themselves, arms outstretched, for a full body hug, and his response is to wag his tail and — I swear — hug them back.

We waited until we moved into our home, and on December 7th 2012, Booker was scheduled on a flight from Calgary to Houston, and then Houston to Philadelphia. It was going to be a long day for him, but United assured me that he would be allowed out of his crate in Houston for a walk.

The evening before his journey, I posted an excited message on Facebook:

Tomorrow, after being separated from Booker for over a year, he will be coming back to live with us. Poor puppy has a long day tomorrow. He will be picked up at 4:30 am and fly from Calgary to Houston where he will be able to get out of his kennel for a pee break and some water. Then back in for the flight from Houston to Philadelphia. We pick him up around 10:00 pm. Then we'll be working to get him over the trauma of being uprooted from his Calgary "pack".

The weather that day was as beautiful as it gets in Calgary in December. It was a balmy 7 Celsius or 19 Fahrenheit, when they loaded him on the plane at 6 a.m. Then for some unknown reason, the flight was delayed. 6 a.m. became 7 a.m., then 9 a.m. and finally, at noon, the plane left for Houston.

122

The connecting flight was missed, so Booker was unloaded and put in the warehouse somewhere in Houston. I say *somewhere* since they never could tell me where he was.

At 5 p.m they called to tell me that he was on the earlier flight, and I could pick him up in Philadelphia at 10 p.m., which would have been great, but I already received an email telling me the delay of the first flight meant he couldn't make the second flight.

My frantic calls to find my dog were met with indifference. One customer service rep responded to my, "Oh my goodness, you've lost my dog" with "We haven't lost your dog ma'am, we just can't locate him right now". If I hadn't been so upset I would have laughed. She was, however, able to confirm that he wasn't on the earlier flight.

A few of the people I talked to were concerned and compassionate, and tried to help as much as they could, but there didn't seem to be a consistent policy for dealing with a lost pet.

United PetSafe received a failing grade in all five of my Tenets: Caring, Consistency, Competence, Commitment and Communication.

Finally at 12:30 p.m., we were able to go to the United Cargo in Philadelphia, and pick Booker up. He had been in the crate for over 18 hours.

When he saw us he stood up and excitedly wagged his tail. I'm amazed at his sweetness and vowed that I would never put him on another plane.

United says this about their pet travel policy:

"United PetSafe offers airport-to-airport travel for cats and dogs, traveling to approximately 300 destinations. Members of our PetSafe team are trained professionals, who love animals, and are dedicated to ensuring that all pets receive the best care throughout their entire journey."

Like Dave Carroll, I never received an apology, explanation, follow-up, or compensation for the nightmare we went through with our dog.

Johnson & Johnson engendered huge trust, and the management of United continues to lose it.

Chapter 8

BUILDING TRUST THROUGH EMOTIONAL INTELLIGENCE

I studied emotional intelligence, sometimes called EQ or EI (we use the terms interchangeably), for over a decade. My work around trust was a result of my deep curiosity, about how the two are connected. Why do different people witness the same person doing exactly the same thing, and arrive at different conclusions as to their trustworthiness? How can a person who is cruel and lies to others still believe *they* were trusted? I have learned that there are times when people really aren't aware of how they are coming across to others. It comes down to emotional intelligence.

I first read Daniel Goleman's book, *Emotional Intelligence*, in 1998. At that time there wasn't a test to measure EI, so when I found that a company in Canada had developed one, I jumped at the chance to be certified and use it in my consulting work. The more I read and studied, the more excited I got and wanted to learn more.

I went to my first conference on emotional intelligence in 2000, in California, where I met and talked to Dr. Peter Salovey. Dan Goleman credited him and Dr. Jack Mayer as the pioneering psychologists, who originally coined the term and the study. It piqued my interest, and set me off on a journey that has, so far, lasted over 15 years.

Years of certifications, classes, books, white papers, and attending conferences around the world eventually led to me co-chairing an international conference, and then progress to speaking at conferences around the world, sharing the stage with some of the people I had studied with.

Here is my own definition of emotional intelligence:

Emotional Intelligence is our ability to:

- **Accurately identify emotions in ourselves and others**
- **Understand and manage emotions**
- **Use and effectively communicate emotional feelings**

— Lea Brovedani

I've often been asked if emotional intelligence is something people could use to manipulate others. It's such an interesting question that I put it out to the greatest authorities and experts around. Yes — my friends on Facebook!

All jokes aside, some of my associates on Facebook are truly authorities in emotional intelligence, and it's the quickest way to get an opinion from them.

My colleague and friend, Matt Perelstein, has been doing great work in the field of emotional intelligence for over 30 years. When I posed the question to him, this is what he had to say:

"Definitely! EQ is about consciously manipulating conversations, relationships, and interactions to a better place, on purpose. I've called us many times, *master manipulators*. But like another colleague said, if it's win-win, then it's EQ. If it's win-lose, then no."

By answering the way he did, Matt used his knowledge of emotional intelligence and immediately disarmed the sting of the question. That wasn't what I expected him to say, but it was brilliant, and I learned as much from *how* he answered as *what* he answered. The general consensus from the group of EQ practitioners was that a high EQ person would use what they know of emotional intelligence for the general good of society, and the result is greater trust all around.

"People will remember the emotion of the situation long after they have forgotten the words and deeds, and their trust is affected by the emotions they feel."
- Lea Brovedani -

127

Emotional Intelligence and Trust

	Reflective Questions	Skills and Concepts
Identify Emotions	How do you recognize emotions? Where do you hold emotions in your body? *How do you know for sure that what you believe is true?*	**Be empathetic:** Pick up on emotional and social cues to react appropriately. Work to understand others, read body language and other nonverbal communication **Self-honesty:** Accept your own qualities and faults, and recognize your own patterns of behavior that help and hinder situations. **Recognize that your own emotions can get in the way of accurately accessing emotions in others.**
Understand and Manage	Will your response help or hinder the situation? Can you increase your awareness of your actions so that you see their effects? Are you hearing the unspoken messages?	**Reason and motivation:** Weigh your decisions and behavior by identifying and prioritizing what is important. **Manage feelings:** Use simple techniques, like a pause for reflection, to act – not react. **Choose to affirm the positive:** Accept that you have choice, can make a difference, and are an important part of the community. **Develop social behaviors:** Respond to people's needs; build conflict resolution skills; accept feedback. **Interdependence:** Recognize your place in the larger community; your awareness and decision making takes into account the short and long term consequences of your actions, as well as the context/culture.
Use and Communicate	What is this emotion telling you? Do you know how to use emotional language to help understanding? Are you healing or hurting? What effect will your emotional reaction have on others? Will this emotion help you reach your goal?	**Apply consequential thinking:** Evaluate cause and effect; anticipate outcomes; **Empathy:** Use your compassionate awareness to guide your choices. **Express emotions appropriately.** **Practice integrity:** Hold yourself to high standards and do what is right – even when it seems hopeless.

How we trust others is tied up with our emotions. Being able to understand our own emotions and those of others is an important aspect of our trustability.

Can Trust Be Learned?

When I decided to create a workshop on trust, I partnered with a colleague I admire and trust. Chuck Wolfe is considered one of the top experts on training in emotional intelligence, and it's no surprise that he is also highly regarded by his peers. He is a member of the prestigious Consortium for Research on EI in Organizations, as well as being on the advisory board and training committee for the International Society of Emotional Intelligence.

I was initially intimidated by Chuck, not for anything he said or did, since he really is a great guy to work with, but because heck, he is one of the top EI people in the world! After all, Dr. Peter Salovey, President of Yale University, Dr. Jack Mayer of the University of New Hampshire, and Dr. David Carusco chose Chuck to help write the training program for the Mayers, Salovey, Carusco Emotional Intelligence Test (MSCEIT), an abilities-based assessment of emotional intelligence. They were pioneers of the emotional intelligence movement.

It didn't take long to become comfortable, though, as we dove into creating experiential exercises to give participants the ah-ha's that would provide them with new insights into trust.

I loved the first exercise Chuck created to start the journey. We called it "Where Do You Start with Trust?"

We had participants identify where they start in trusting others in a work context, and had them imagine being introduced to another person who was new to the company. They had to determine if they start from a position of no trust, represented by number one, total trust, represented by number ten, or some number in between. They were told to write that number down.

Now participants had to stand up and go stand along the wall, underneath the number they had chosen.

Illustration by Phillip Brovedani

Once they were there, they were asked to share with people closest to them why they had chosen that number.

What was found was that there were one or two at the beginning and end of the line representing either a one or a ten, but most people were towards the middle. It's a simple exercise that so brilliantly shows that we can start from different places of trust, and it opened the conversation between the participants that chose the number one or the number ten on what they each needed to do in order to improve trust.

Let's dive into why EQ and trust are connected.

Which person do you respect the most? Who's the best boss you've ever had? What friend do you love spending time with?

Make a list of the reasons. How many of them would fall under the *soft* skills, and how many would you list as *hard* skills?

Soft skills are sometimes hard to quantify, but they include all the skills around getting along with others; showing that you are caring, listening, being polite, managing anger, and generally persuading others to listen and relate to you.

Hard skills are more specific teachable abilities that can be defined and measured. Skills like typing, building a house, math,

130

science — anything that can be quantified — is usually a hard skill.

If you are like many of the people who have participated in my classes, the answer comes down to their EQ, which definitely falls under the soft skills.

Organizational EI

I'm a member of the Canadian Association of Professional Speakers (CAPS). It has been my privilege to be part of the organization for over 10 years, and I've served as President of a local chapter on the east coast of Canada. What has delighted me is the number of truly honorable and trustworthy people I've met through CAPS.

The organization is founded on the principles of an American speaker by the name of Cavett Robert. Cavett formed the National Speakers Association in the United States when the speaking profession was in its infancy. His motto was: "Don't worry about how we divide up the pie — there is enough for everybody. Let's just make a bigger pie!"

Within the organization I've met and made lifelong friends with some of the world's top speakers. I've been delighted to find out that they are also some of the most emotionally intelligent, likeable, and honorable people you could meet.

When I'm looking for people to partner with, or to hire a reputable coach, I first look at the CAPS membership list. I know the high standards they hold people to, and if someone is found acting or behaving unethically, they are barred from the organization.

Tom Stoyan exemplifies all the best that CAPS promises. He is a former college professor, and one of the founding members of

CAPS. I've taken a number of the webinars Tom has provided free of charge to CAPS members. He is known as *Canada's Sales Coach,* so it's not that he isn't in big demand and does these free webinars to fill his time. He believes that when he helps others to succeed, we all benefit, so he finds the time. When I hear the words integrity and respect, I think of him.

Tom made sure we all understood that the best salespeople are the ones who care about their clients. To *find out what their pain, passion, or purpose is,* then find the solution you have that fills that need. Tom teaches that it isn't about pushing products or solutions on someone who doesn't need them, but finding out what the client needs, and getting it for them.

He would walk away from a sale if he didn't believe he was the right fit, or had the right product for them; and he encourages those he teaches to do the same thing. Tom cares deeply about others and that (plus his high integrity) makes him someone I trust and listen to. That trust is extended to people he recommends, and a referral from Tom is gold, since many others feel the same way about him.

Rotary Club

I've presented at the Rotary club, and trust most of the people I meet in the organization. I have used their 4-way test to decide whether or not to repeat something I've heard, or give an opinion to someone.

The Four-Way Test

1. Is it the TRUTH?
2. Is it FAIR to all concerned?
3. Will it build GOODWILL and BETTER FRIENDSHIPS?
4. Will it be BENEFICIAL to all concerned?

I can't help but believe that social media would be very quiet if everyone invoked the four-way test before they posted anything online.

The Surgeon

I was working as a coach for a brilliant young surgeon. A formal complaint of bullying had been lodged against her by one of the medical school students, and patients found her cold and uncaring. Her hospital took the charges seriously, and she had to change her behavior or risk being fired.

When she walked me through her day, I was amazed at the frenetic pace she had to keep in order to accomplish her tasks. She was brilliant, and in the time it would take most people to look at a problem, she had looked at it, analyzed it, and figured out a course of action.

She was impatient with students, and wasn't above yelling at them if they made a mistake. In her mind, there were lives at stake, and mistakes shouldn't be tolerated at all.

We began our work together by setting her goals. She knew what she didn't want. She didn't want to be fired, and she didn't want patients constantly calling her during the week with "stupid" questions. By helping her flip those negatives into positives, we came up with two goals.

1. She wanted to be a respected, trusted member of the Senior Medical Team.

2. She wanted to have more time to do research during the week.

I asked her to describe a typical round visiting the patients. She told me she would walk in, check their charts, consult with the attending physician, then tell the patient, as succinctly and

133

quickly as possible, what they could expect in their treatment plan. Slam, bam, thank you ma'am, and we're done!

Because of the large number of patients she had to see, she tried to keep her visit to less than five minutes. After some brainstorming, I asked if she would be willing to stretch her five minutes to six minutes, and test that out for a week.

Although she was extremely competent, she showed very little care. I tasked her with just smiling at a patient when she walked in, and to make it as genuine as possible. I also had her ask at the end whether they had any questions. She said that would make her visit longer than six minutes, and she wasn't very pleased with my suggestion! Her career was on the line, so she promised to try it for the week, and report back to me.

She was amazed to discover that she saved hours during the week because patients and their advocates weren't calling her demanding to know more. Reassuring her patients and taking time to answer questions while she was in their rooms was a pivotal moment in her career. As brilliant as she was, she didn't realize what her "efficiency" cost her.

Like our good doctor, if you are a leader who knows that there are important changes coming that you absolutely have to get people to accept, there are a few things you need to do.

First, you need to allow people the time to process the information and lay things out as problems that need to be solved. We process problems in a different area of the brain than change that is forced upon us.

Give people an opportunity to discuss the situation, and recognize that emotional issues take longer to accept. The doctor knew she had to change, but it felt painful, and she had trouble taking direction from people she didn't feel were as smart as she was. We had to find ways to set goals and come up with ways to meet them together.

134

The best time to get people to accept change is before the change is necessary. Wouldn't it have been great if emotional intelligence were one of the core classes when she was starting out in a profession that is supposed to heal and care?

A great leader encourages staff to look at potential problems and brainstorm solutions. The worst time is during the catastrophe when emotions are high. Don't try to hide or run away from the problem.

As I've said before, communicate openly. Be transparent. People can sniff out deceit, and those problems you thought you were avoiding by hiding them are going to blow up, and you'll have more complications than you can handle.

Be empathetic and listen to how people are feeling. Reassure first before giving them the facts. Throwing facts at people is like throwing bricks through a window with messages attached. They might get there quickly, but they're not going to make the recipient feel good about what they learn, and will probably get you the opposite of what you want.

A Tale of Two Dentists

When I had dental surgery, someone made a mistake that resulted in an inconvenience that — seriously — will not even be something I remember a week from now. OK maybe it will now that I'm writing about it! When all the smoke cleared, apologies were given and received, I realized that the office I trusted the most was the one that had made the mistake.

WARNING – Graphic description of tooth pain!

I was flossing my teeth when the dental floss got stuck under a cap. When I gave a tug, the tooth broke off at the root, and flew across the bathroom floor. I went down on my hands and knees and found it next to the shower — another five inches to the left and it would have been a slam-dunk in the toilet and been lost forever!

Since that tooth had undergone a root canal it didn't hurt, but I knew seeing the jagged remains of the root wasn't a good thing, and it was going to be an expensive repair.

I made a dentist appointment as soon as possible, and went, cap in hand, to see what he could do for me.

He laid out the possibilities, and together we decided that the best option was to have the roots extracted, and put in a dental implant. I could hear the *ka-ching* sound as he explained what needed to be done.

Two weeks later, I was lying in the dental surgeon's chair, draped in an antiseptic gown, with a matching cap, and my mouth wedged open. He asked if I would mind if the new office manager could observe the surgery, and I gave my consent with the muffled "yes" that dentists can somehow decipher.

I was glad I brought my headphones to listen to music that drowned out the sound of the scraping, pulling, and drilling that was reverberating in my skull. Every once in a while, I would hear the surgeon describing what he was doing, and I turned the music up. I really didn't want to know.

When he was finished, he gave me a positive, "You did great Lea", before sending me on my way. When I was walking out the door, I saw that he was still in a deep conversation with the office manager.

Their office had offered to call my husband twenty minutes before surgery was done to pick me up, so I was annoyed when I got downstairs to see no car waiting for me. When I called my husband, he told me he hadn't received a call. I sat on a bench outside the office, silently cursing, and holding an ice pack to my swollen jaw.

I was supposed to go from the surgeon to my dentist, to be fitted with a flipper — a false tooth that can be inserted, while they wait for the graft and bone to heal around the implant. The freezing started to come out, and all that talk about it not hurting at all was no longer true. It hurt! A lot!

When I called my dentist to ask about waiting to get the false tooth inserted in my throbbing jaw, there was silence for a moment. "That should have been done. We had it sent to the dental surgeon. We'll call their office and see why they didn't do it."

The surgeon's office called and apologized profusely. They told me to come back to their office right away, so they could insert the tooth, and do any adjustments so I wouldn't have to make two trips — one to them, and the other to my dentist.

We were leaving to go on a trip to a friend's cottage that afternoon, and being cranky, pained, and ready to leave, I gave them a very definitive "NO". I'd get it done when I came back. After all, I thought, I could be in pain anywhere, so why not choose someplace I enjoy? As crazy as it sounds, it was the right decision. The beautiful scenery and relaxing atmosphere took my mind off the discomfort.

When I returned from my holiday at the cottage, I was pleasantly surprised to see that my dentist had texted me an appointment reminder for the following Monday. Great! Everything was taken care of, but just to be sure I wrote them a message the night before my appointment, confirming that they had the tooth. For some reason, my intuition told me to also call the dentist's office and confirm. When I did, the receptionist told me I didn't have an appointment.

The office manager came on the phone and started the conversation with, "When you missed the first appointment, this one was cancelled." I hadn't missed the appointment. They had cancelled it, and I mentioned that quite emphatically. She went on to tell me that her office had not made any mistakes; the fault lay with the other office. I'm not proud of the fact that I swore, and when I got off the phone it took me a few minutes to calm down. Her last, condescending words to me were, "You have a nice day," which just infuriated me even more.

Within the hour, I received a call from the surgeon's office, and the first thing they said was, "We don't blame you for being upset. We want to tell you it was all our mistake. We are so sorry, and can assure you this isn't how we run our business. You let us know when you are available to come in."

When I arrived at their office the surgeon who had done the surgery walked in, shook my hand and said "Lea, none of this was the fault of the other office. I take entire responsibility for messing up and can assure you it won't happen again."

So at the end of this long saga, I found that only one of the offices made a mistake. As I've said over and over again, it's not the mistake that made the difference, but how they handled it. One office was intent on making sure I was okay, and went out of their way to apologize. The other went out of their way to make sure I knew they were right, but didn't pick up on any cues that I was upset. Which one had the higher EI, and which one would you trust?

So much of customer service comes down to whether or not you trust that they care about you.

Lack of trust slows things down

When trust is low, it takes longer to complete business transactions — or they're not completed at all. We take more time checking and double-checking information, strategies, and suggestions.

One way you can raise emotional intelligence in your organization is to start asking people how they feel. Insist on getting feelings as the response, not thoughts disguised as feelings. (Examples of thoughts in disguise: *I feel like..., I feel that..., I feel as if...*)

Here are some steps to follow:

Step 1

Start with their feelings. Ask them specifically, on a scale of 0-10, how much they feel
- Respected
- Appreciated
- Supported

When the number is less than 10, ask (or figure out) what it would take to raise the numbers. ***Then do it.***

Next, ask how much they feel
- Criticized
- Controlled

Ask what it would take to lower the numbers.

If you have a large organization you're not going to be able to ask every single person, but you need to find a way to obtain the information.

Then take action.

Step 2

Start expressing your own feelings. Begin sentences with:
I am afraid....
I feel confused about...

I appreciate...
I feel concerned about...

Again, don't confuse expressing your feeling with stating an opinion or lecturing. If you say *I feel that…,* you are giving them an opinion. If you say *I feel you should…,* you are giving a directive or lecturing. **Be authentic and honest in expressing your feelings.**

Step 3

After expressing your feelings, let your employees figure out what to do. Don't tell them. Don't underestimate their intelligence and rob them of a chance to feel good about themselves.

Let go of control.

Step 4

Start thinking about the impact your words have on their feelings. Remember, people do their best work when they feel good about themselves.

Respect them.

This may be a new way of thinking for you, and it will take practice. The reward is greater trust within your organization.

What we can learn about EI from soldiers

The first time I taught at a military base, I was nervous. I didn't know what to expect, and my image of the military was based on way too many movies in which soldiers carried out orders without question, and didn't seem to have a sense of humor. I was watching the wrong movies obviously.

The enlisted people I met, both men and women, were wonderful. The added bonus that I discovered, over the years I spent facilitating workshops on the base, is they were respectful, punctual, and had a wickedly fun and sarcastic wit. They didn't blindly follow orders, or accept what they were told without question. They had a lot of questions, and I learned as much as I taught.

When I was teaching a program on emotional intelligence at St. Mary's University, in Halifax, I had a really eclectic group. There was one politician, a social worker, a number of middle and senior managers from real estate, and a special operations soldier, who wasn't even supposed to be there but was substituting for a Captain, who had originally signed on. Andre was from Quebec, and spoke with a charming French Canadian accent. He also gave me one of the best testimonials I've ever had.

He told me this: "Lea, when I was told that I had to attend this workshop, I thought, 'Okay, it will be a break from duties. I'll sit through this crap and take notes for my Captain.' But Lea", he said. "This is not crap. Everyone should take it!" I laughed and told him that his "This is not crap" compliment was the best testimonial I'd ever received.

Months before, I had presented my program on the base, and his Captain hadn't been able to attend because of prior engagements, but had signed up for my program at the University. I had spoken to him on a number of occasions, and felt he would bring a lot of his own intelligence, questions, and value to the class. I was a little disappointed when I found out he couldn't attend. Instead he sent his "This is not crap" soldier in his stead.

On the first day of the class, Andre didn't contribute to any of the dialogue. He participated, but it was more of a respectful, and very limited contribution; answering questions with short monosyllabic answers. If this kept up, it would have been a boring week. I'm happy to say that by end of the 5 days, Andre was all-in. I was so glad that he was part of the group.

As part of the Special Forces in the Canadian military, he was deployed in dangerous situations to protect Canada from threats, save people in catastrophes, and recover bodies when the worst happened. In 1968, the Royal Canadian Navy, the Canadian Army, and the Royal Canadian Air Force were combined into one service: the Canadian Armed Forces. Andre went where he was needed regardless of where it was, but most of his time was spent in the navy.

He couldn't share much of what he did, but he did share a rescue operation that made the news. He had to dive in dangerous waters, and help bring up the remains of victims, who were killed when Swiss Air flight 111 went down, off the coast of Nova Scotia in 1998. I learned this in a quiet conversation we had, and I saw the compassion and respect when he talked of the people who had perished, and could only imagine the horrors he witnessed.

Andre had a wicked sense of humor and wit and when he engaged others in the class. During those times you wouldn't know what he did or saw. Humor helps us deal with whatever we are dealt with in life.

He was one of the first to give me insights into how soldiers develop deep trust through their caring and commitment to each other. Andre told me that trust wasn't just a buzzword. It was critical for safety, teamwork, and operations. In situations that require split second decisions, you have to trust the people you're with, so you aren't wasting time wondering if they have your back.

A Tale of Two Captains

Andre told me the story of the two captains of a ship on which he served. The first captain was respected and liked by all of the men and women onboard. A couple of times a day he would walk throughout the ship and talk to them, exchanging stories, and getting to know things about them. He knew them all by name, would ask them stories about their families, and make comments about the work they were doing.

Those walks took up a few hours, since he stopped and talked to people, and continued conversations from the days and weeks before. Conversations like "How did Kayla's soccer tournament turn out?" or "Has your wife had the baby? Let us know so we can celebrate with you!" Andre said he could tell you something personal about each of the people on the ship, since in the weeks or months of the deployment, he spent time getting to know the men and women who served under him.

People felt that he cared about them as individuals, and didn't just see them for the position they held, or the job they did. Andre's comment was "they would follow him into hell if he asked them."

When he left, he was replaced by the captain Andre called the "Attaboy/Attagirl Captain". When he looked at the soldiers, there was no recognition and no small talk to get to know them as an individuals. Andre said they joked and said he must have had a book that said "At 11 a.m. and 2 p.m., walk around and greet people".

For example, if someone was scrubbing the deck, he would pat them on the shoulder, and say "Attaboy" or "Attagirl", which is how he got his moniker. What he didn't notice was they rolled their eyes, and tightened their lips at the comment many give their dogs when they perform a trick.

At 11 a.m. and 2 p.m. everyday, they would look at their watches and wait for the "Attaboy walk", which was always on time. At least he got high marks for consistency. They didn't feel he really cared about them beyond the job they were doing, and questioned whether he had their best interests at heart.

Everyone I've talked to in the military said the trust relationship with a commanding officer is vitally important. It really does fall into the Five Tenets of Trust; Caring, Commitment, Consistency, Competence and Communication.

Caring is a big part of trust, especially when you are asking people to put their life on the line. Heck, it's important even when it's not a life or death situation. You show care by getting to know people, and seeing them as more than the job they do. It highlighted for me that you can be competent as heck and behave consistently, but you won't establish the trust that you could if people believe you care.

Before I started working with the military, I believed that they had different rules around trust and engagement. I had believed that soldiers blindly followed orders and trusted without question. What I learned was they had to have a high level of trust in order to confidently follow their leaders. It really isn't all that different from what happens in the corporate world.

A Soldier's Story – Benjamin Sledge

Benjamin Sledge was the author of a story that did the rounds of the social media, titled "Today's Problem with Masculinity Isn't What You Think". Benjamin was a former soldier, who served in Afghanistan and Iran. He has first-hand knowledge of the importance of trust in the military. His article is a great piece of writing around masculinity, and touched on why enlisted men and women trust each other. For me, it really enforced how much vulnerability is a part of trust. The gist of the article is that soldiers develop the deep trust and lasting bonds because of the time they spend together, discussing their deepest fears, joys, and hopes. "Of the men I served with, I can tell you about their life stories, fears, victories, relationships, and struggles. We've cried, hugged, laughed, and shared some of our deepest secrets with one another," says Benjamin.

144

I was so taken with the article and Ben's insights into trust that I searched for him online, and asked if he'd consent to an interview.

Ben's perspective is from someone who knows. He fought and served in the military, and he has experienced the deep trust that comes from fighting alongside men who depended on each other to stay alive.

He joined the army in 1999. For some of the men who joined, it was an alternative to continuing a life in gangs and ending up in jail. Some were from areas of the country where there were few opportunities for employment, and the military offered them a job.

For Ben, it was an eye opening experience to meet people from different areas of the United States. He was a middle class kid from the suburbs. In boot camp he met racists from small towns in rural Tennessee and ex-gang members from the inner city of Philadelphia. Somehow, they all had to learn to trust each other and find a way to work as a team.

I was curious. How do you get people with opposite views, from such different backgrounds to work together as a unit? The following is my adaptation of what Ben told me about life in the military.

Imagine an insanely difficult exercise that is close to impossible to achieve. Now, imagine that it doesn't matter how well you do, it depends on how well the team does. If one person fails, everyone fails. If you are the one who causes the team to fail, you not only have to face the punishment from the drill sergeant; you face it from every single person in your platoon.

They also came together over their hatred of the drill sergeant. The concept of "The enemy of my enemy is my friend" gave them a bond that superseded any animosity they would normally have felt for each other.

In basic training, they had to learn creeds and army drills. For one or two whole days they had to scream these creeds at the top of their lungs. A creed is an oath or saying that provides a value structure by which to live or work by.

The drill sergeant would say "You almost had it", but it was never good enough, or they'd say one person wasn't loud enough, and I'd be thinking, "Who is this idiot?"

"They'd exercise us until people were throwing up. It was a horrible experience," says Ben. "After five days, we all figured out that it didn't really matter what we did. It would never be good enough — and yes, we learned that life wasn't fair. Once we figured that out, we learned how to deal with rejections, failure, disappointment, and to keep on going."

In 13 short weeks, men became friends, and on family day, the soldier they nicknamed Tennessee, was introducing his family to his best friend from Compton. Color no longer divided them. Pieces of life were revealed bit by bit, and trust grew as people opened up and became more vulnerable with each other.

It's Not Just in the Heat of Battle

Contrary to what I believed, the deepest trust wasn't developed in the heat of battle. It happened in the quiet times, when they had nothing to do but share a piece of themselves. Sharing stories of their families, their hopes, fears, and discovering common bonds. Comforting each other when they found out that a relationship had ended, crying on each other's shoulders, and showing that they could count on a friend to be there for them.

When Ben found out he was going to be deployed to a dangerous war zone, he was scared. He went to his team leader and begged him, "Don't send me. I'll work at a desk in the office. I'll do anything else." The team sergeant pulled him aside and said,

"Ben, I know you're scared. We're all scared." He took the time to share his own fear, and let Ben know that he was needed in order for the team to succeed. By him opening up and sharing his own fear, Ben learned to trust.

Ben told me that his first sergeant died of cancer last year, and every single one of the men in the platoon showed up at his funeral. All of the people who were with him in Iraq knew he was instrumental in getting everyone through it. When they saw each other, it was as if nothing had changed. They greeted each other like brothers and best friends.

They weren't afraid to cry, hug one another, or share and showed their grief. Many of the soldiers coming home miss the emotional bonding they had, and the loneliness and isolation gets in the way of trust with others who didn't share their experiences in the war.

While most of us don't have to depend on each other for our lives as soldiers do, there is something we can learn from them. Even in the corporate setting, ask yourself these questions:

- Do I have the respect of those who work for me?
- Can others rely on me to do what I say I will do?
- Does my competence instill trust in others?
- Is my communication clear and concise?
- What are the shared values that create a common bond?
- What experiences do I have that others can learn from?
- Can others count on me to support them when things get difficult?
- Am I willing to discuss those areas that could cause problems?

Chapter 9

DON'T HOLD ON TO THE PAST

If you've never made a mistake, then you're either not conscious, or you're not trying hard enough. Most of my greatest lessons in life were from my own mistakes.

You might find it easier to remember other people's mistakes than your own. My friend, colleague, and mentor Dr. Anabel Jensen told me we judge others by their actions, and ourselves by our intentions — but we should do the opposite. Wise words Dr. Jensen.

The Christmas Gift

I chuckle every time I think of the first Christmas my husband and I spent together. We were married at the end of our backpacking trip throughout Africa and Europe. It was also the end of all of the money we had saved to travel, so when we arrived back in Canada, we were broke. We borrowed the first month's rent from our parents, went out, and found jobs. That first year was pretty lean, trying to furnish a place, pay rent, and pay back what we borrowed.

At Christmas, we agreed that our purchase of a microwave would be a big present for us both. The way I interpreted this was that we weren't to buy each other a big gift. No expensive presents — but little gifts were still expected. I guess I just assumed that Ric would know this without me having to tell him. I've learned that people don't *just know*. You have to tell them.

Christmas morning came. Our first Christmas as a married couple, I ran to the tree and grabbed the small presents I had wrapped for Ric. "Open this one first," I said, barely able to contain my excitement. Each gift I had bought for him was wrapped beautifully; new gloves, after-shave, a batch of favorite cookies, his favorite bar of chocolate, each one picked with thought and care. I had been gathering small gifts to wrap for weeks. With each gift he opened his look of pain became more pronounced.

"I thought we agreed, no gifts," Ric said sheepishly.

There wasn't anything for me under the tree. Not a card, not a box of chocolates — nothing. With a hurt look I said "We said no *big* gifts." He's never made that mistake again!

Small misunderstandings can build into big trust issues, if you let them. For good or bad, I share how I feel, and this was no exception. It's something I learned early in my work in emotional intelligence; You start by sharing your feelings.

"*I feel…*"
and then a feeling word.
"I feel sad."

"*I feel like…*"
We often complete the sentence with a behavior or thing
"*I feel like going out.*"

"*I feel that…*"
We are expressing a thought or an opinion, rather than a feeling
"*I feel that you aren't listening.*"

When I shared with Ric that I felt unvalued and unloved, he gave me a big hug and apologized. He also let me talk it out, and showed me that he heard what I had to say.

Over the years we've continued to work at our communication. He's taught me never to say, "We need to talk", which makes him want to run, screaming from the room. I've taught him — Oh, heck! I just don't have enough pages (hahaha).

Whether it's a business or personal situation, in order to trust, you have to have open and honest communication.

Letting Go

I've noticed that letting go in business is the same process as letting go of a bad relationship. You have to want to let go.

In the mid-'90s, my husband was working for a boss, who actively disliked him. As Ric was the sole breadwinner for our family, he put up with a lot of verbal abuse and criticism, thinking that he could keep his head down, work hard, and ride it out.

Day by day, and week by week, I could see him retreat into himself, and spend more time sitting in front of the TV, becoming more depressed, as he tried to deal with the bullying he was experiencing at the office. Our small children and I were ignored, as he dealt with the stress of being constantly criticized and berated.

After a year, the new manager found a reason to fire Ric, and the reason was so lame it would have been easy to sue the company for wrongful dismissal. I wanted to hire a lawyer and fight, but Ric realized that every moment fighting was another day spent in the muck. He chose to let go and move on.

I'm not saying you should always let injustices go, but for Ric and me, this was the right decision. The first thing Ric did was take some time off to reconnect with us. I went from being the stay-at-home Mom to being the primary wage earner, and he spent a summer laughing and connecting with his children. It was the best thing that could have happened to all of us, but it never would have happened if he hadn't been willing to let go.

A good friend of mine left a business relationship under the same circumstances. Like Ric, she had the experience of working with a Jekyll and Hyde. You may know this character in the story by Robert Louis Stevenson, about a man with a split personality: one good and one evil. Like the story, my friend never knew by looking at the person which character she was going to have to deal with.

In the beginning, Linda looked around and liked what she saw. After raising a family and being newly single, she was ready for new adventures and opportunities, and saw the potential for building a business, in a new market, at an exotic locale. She was sold on the promise of being able to run the business in her own way, with financial support, while she built the client base. They agreed that it would take a couple of years to take it to its full potential.

It wasn't long before she saw a few things that concerned her. Her new partner complained about all her staff, without exception. She attributed any successes to her own work, and any problems to the incompetence of others. She was great at managing up, and heaped compliments on the COO in public, but privately disparaged him.

Although they had discussed the time it would take to launch the business, if a proposal wasn't successful, she would angrily berate Linda and call her names. One moment she would be saying "You're ruining my business. You don't know what you are doing, and I should never have brought you in." In the next breath, if things went well, she would be praising and lavishing compliments, saying how happy she was with their partnerships. Criticisms were a blunt instrument, used to justify her mercurial mood. If she was in a bad mood, it was the fault of the incompetent people she had to support.

After two years of working with this person, Linda left. It took her a couple of months before she got over feeling the effects of the abuse.

It's Not Fair

Maybe you feel that the situation you are in isn't fair.

My friend Kym Shegog-Ramsey is a successful businesswoman, entrepreneur, philanthropist and an awesome Mom to three very talented daughters. I've heard her say, "Once you realize life isn't fair, you start to succeed."

I wonder if it is something she learned when she was a captain in the military. It is similar to what Benjamin Karp told me when I interviewed him. They were taught to move beyond what is fair, and deal with what is happening.

Online sites like *PyschCentral* and *Psychology Today* talk about the steps you can take to move on.

1. Make the decision to let it go

You have a choice here. You have to consciously decide you aren't going to let it rule your life. Reliving all the details keeps you in that negative spot, and stymies your ability to move forward. I have friends who have gone through horrible moments in their lives, and the ones who succeed made the decision not to let them dictate their future.

2. Express Your Pain and Your Responsibility

It might feel good to cast yourself as the hero to another person's villain, but in some way you had a part to play. What part of the problem can you take responsibility for?

Express the pain, hurt, and disappointment directly to the other person. If that isn't possible, talk to someone who will listen. Get it out of your system.

I've noticed Ric can talk about something once, and it seems to be gone. I need to talk about it *ad nauseam* until it no longer holds energy for me, and saying it out loud helps me discover what it really is that bothers me. For me, that is a longer process.

3. Don't let your pain become your identity

In the late 1960s there was a television show called *Queen for a Day*. The show focused on women, down on their luck, and without much hope. The studio audience voted for the woman with the most compelling and pathetic story, and she was crowned *Queen for a Day*.

Producer, Howard Blake, called it *poverty porn* and said that it was the worst program on television. Between the times on the radio show, where it originated, and the television show, it ran for 24 years, and was the most popular program of the era.

The women who were on this program were desperate, and their stories were ones of despair. The only people who could watch were the upper middle class who could afford televisions at that time. It was really about the exploitation of misery. Their pain became their identity and, as we know, we don't rise up if we identify with being down. Do you want to be identified as the victim or the survivor?

If you live in self-limiting beliefs, you will limit your present and your future.

4. Focus on the present

When you are focused on making the present as good as it can be, you have less time to dwell in the past.

Mindfulness exercises are great for helping you stay focused in the present. When we are mindful, we are fully in the present moment, and not reliving what happened in the past or what could happen in the future.

A mindfulness exercise you can do is to spend a few moments concentrating on your breath. Try it. Take a breath in through your nose, and feel your belly expand. See if you can inhale to a slow count of five. Now, slowly exhale through your mouth to a count of 10. Do this a few times but make sure you are seated, and in a safe place, just in case you feel dizzy.

If you find yourself drifting back to what occurred, try giving yourself a conscious cue. You can say to yourself "I survived and learned. It has passed, and now I can _____".

5. Forgive

Forgive yourself. Forgive others. It's not about just saying "it's okay", especially if you feel the behavior was reprehensible. It's about letting go of the pain.

Forgiveness is not for the weak. It takes strength and courage to forgive, and it allows us to release a blackness of the soul that can take up a lot of room.

> "It takes a strong person to say sorry,
> and an ever stronger person to forgive."
> -Anonymous-

We all make mistakes. The people who are most trusted are usually the people who trust the most. In order to continue trusting, you have to be willing to make a leap of faith. That requires you to be open to vulnerability, risk taking, and not knowing. I know it's not easy, but only when you embrace the leap can you be open to trusting again.

Truly forgiving takes patience and determination, until whatever hurt you no longer holds energy. If you are having trouble letting go and forgiving, find someone who can help you through your anger and grief.

Forgiveness is not about them — it's about you.

> "Hanging onto resentment is letting someone
> you despise live rent-free in your head."
> -Esther Lederer (Ann Landers)-

We may never receive the apology we want, or the emotional release we long for. If you are waiting for them to tell you that you were right, and they were wrong, you may be waiting forever. You have to decide if you are going to let this affect the way you live your life. Bitterness has a way of eating at the person who holds it, not the person who caused it.

Your capacity to forgive and have empathy will affect how well you can trust. Holding on to past hurts can become an excuse for not trusting again. Whenever you find yourself in a victim mentality, give your head a shake! Take your power back, and realize that you have a responsibility to live your best life, with trust and love, regardless of what happens to you.

Chapter 10

TRUST, BUT VERIFY

When he set out to negotiate with Mikhail Gorbachev, Ronald Reagan was advised to learn a few proverbs as Russians like to talk in proverbs. One proverb that he learned was *Trust but verify*, and he used it so often, it is now permanently associated with Reagan.

The world is awash with stories that aren't true, and it is a challenge to know what is real and what is an outright lie. What is fact? What is opinion? What is a belief? And is a fact even a fact when people can see the same thing differently?

It's like throwing all the clean and dirty laundry into the same pile. After a while you don't know which shirt you should wear, because they all stink.

Trust but verify
-Russian Proverb-

The Internet, particularly social media, is the laundry pile for washed and unwashed information. After a while, it all seems to stink, so we have to know what we can wear that is clean and makes us look good. I've been caught passing on information I thought was true when it wasn't, and since I am known as *The Trust Architect,* that just stinks. I absolutely must, and will be someone others can trust. The fact that I was duped is no excuse, and now I check before I repeat information. If I can't verify, or didn't see what occurred with my own eyes, I don't pass it on. I've worked for myself for over 20 years, and I believe in what I teach others. That means I follow my Five Tenets of Trust: Caring, Commitment, Consistency, Competence and Communication.

The Conference

For many years, I've spoken at the same national conference, and I've always found I get business from people who attend my workshop. It's always held in a great location, and is one of the best run conferences I've presented at. Normally, they don't pay their speakers, but this is my business, and regardless of how much I love what I do, a girl's gotta eat.

We've agreed on an amount that works for both of us, which is paid as an honorarium that is less than my usual fee, plus all my expenses. One year, I trusted that our deal for the previous year was understood, and signed the agreement, even though it didn't list the honorarium.

Guess what! I got exactly what the contract stated. I know the organization, and they didn't do this maliciously or with intent to defraud. I trusted them, but with hundreds of speakers to deal with, they didn't remember every contract. If I had verified, I would have had more money in my bank account.

The Internet — What can you Trust?

The great thing about the Internet is that you can research everything online. The horrible thing about the Internet is that you can research everything online! It's like the Wild West, and the onus is on you to make sure the information you're getting is trustworthy.

I've been taken in by false stories on the Internet. Have you? If the story comes from someone I trust, I'm more likely to assume that it's true and pass it on, but I've learned to check the source before I do. As *The Trust Architect*, I don't want to be someone who spreads falsehoods, and I've learned a few ways to discern what is real. Here are some tips to help you do the same.

Look at the Internet address where you are getting your information. Does it end *in .org, .com, .biz, .net, .gov, .mil, .ngo, .info,* or *.edu?*

- **com** – commercial
- **org** – organizations
- **edu** – educational
- **gov** – government
- **net** – network infrastructure
- **mil** – military
- **nom** – private person
- **ngo**– NGOs (Non governmental organization) – a non profit, voluntary citizens' group
- **info** – information

If they are educational, government, military, NGO or information sites, it is more likely the information is true. Websites that end in .com, .biz, .net or a country code (like .co for Columbia) are commercial, and have a product or service to market. It can get even more confusing if it is registered with the country code, since now you have even more domain names to contend with.

So now you know a little more about the sites based on their addresses, but that still doesn't tell you the complete story. If you want to pass on trustworthy information you have to dig a little deeper. Research the name of the organization and the writer. How long have they been around? There are a number of sites that specifically check out stories and tell you whether or not they can be verified — but even these sites need to be vetted.

According to ISTE (International Society for Technology in Education) the following are the top ten sites for checking facts:

> "**AllSides**. While not a fact-checking site, AllSides collects stories from right, center, and left-leaning media so that readers can easily compare how bias influences reporting on each topic. Readers rate the media on a five-point scale,

from far left, left, center, right, and far right. You can see how different media write about the same situation from different perspectives.

"**Fact Check**. This nonpartisan, nonprofit project of the Annenberg Public Policy Center of the University of Pennsylvania monitors the factual accuracy of what is said by U.S. political players, including politicians, TV ads, debates, interviews, and news releases.

"**Media Matters**. This nonprofit, and self-described liberal-leaning research center, monitors and corrects conservative misinformation in the media.

"**NewsBusters**. A project of the conservative Media Research Center, *NewsBusters* is focused on 'documenting, exposing and neutralizing liberal media bias'.

"**Open Secrets**. This nonpartisan, independent, and nonprofit website run by the Center for Responsive Politics tracks how much and where candidates get their money.

"**Politifact**. This Pulitzer Prize winning website rates the accuracy of claims by elected officials. Run by editors and reporters from the independent newspaper *Tampa Bay Times*, *Politicfact* features the Truth-O-Meter, that rates statements as "True," "Mostly True," "Half True," "False," and "Pants on Fire."

"**ProPublica**. This independent, nonprofit newsroom has won several Pulitzer Prizes, including the 2016 Prize for Explanatory Reporting. *ProPublica* produces investigative journalism in the public interest.

"**Snopes**. This independent, nonpartisan website run by professional researcher and writer, David Mikkelson, researches urban legends and other rumors. It is often the first to set the facts straight on wild, fake news claims.

"The Sunlight Foundation. This nonpartisan, nonprofit organization uses public policy data-based journalism to make politics more transparent and accountable.

"Washington Post Fact Checker. Although the *Washington Post* has a left-center bias, its checks are excellent and sourced. The bias shows up because they fact-check conservative claims more than liberal ones."

When I looked into fact-checking sites other than those above, I found many that looked legitimate, but weren't. There were sites that discredited fact-checking sites, so it's no wonder people are confused, and believe that everything is "fake".

Before you retweet, share, or post, do some investigating. Here are some suggestions:

1. Look into the organization and the writer to see if they are legitimate. Is the author of the article well known and respected?
2. How does the information compare with reliable news sources? If no one else has reported it, then do a deeper check.
3. Look for biases. Check for conflicts of interest. (Example: Is the source reporting that soft drinks are the key to longevity a supplier to that industry?)
4. Search for links and citations that support the claims made by the writer and verify them. Look for a couple of credible sources that can support the information.

If you're not willing to do any of this because it's too much work, then don't retweet, share or post the information.

Check your own biases

We often believe stories that come from people we trust, and as young children we trust what our parents tell us. I was raised in a small town that didn't have a lot of diversity, and all my friends came from families that looked the same as mine. My parents were loving, kind people who were a product of their times and of their surroundings. They made jokes and comments about other nationalities, races, and anyone who was of a different religion or sexual orientation, and I believe it was because they never met people who could open their minds to another way of thinking.

I first challenged the beliefs they passed on to me when I was in Grade 2, but it was years later when I started to really question the bigotry I grew up with, and realized I didn't agree with everything I was taught. As I started traveling and meeting people from all walks and ways of life, I saw and met some I liked, and some I didn't. What I liked or didn't like had nothing to do with their appearance, religion, or political belief, and everything to do with their character.

As an impressionable 7-year old, I watched a short movie called *After You, My Dear Alphonse*, which was based on a story written by Shirley Jackson for The New Yorker in 1943.

A young boy named Johnny brings his friend, Boyd, home for lunch. The two boys laugh and talk to each other without any concept of differences. They take turns going first, and do deep bows saying "After you, my dear Alphonse" to each other before going through the door, sharing food or playing with a toy.

When the mother meets Johnny's young friend, Boyd, she is surprised that he is from another race, and her demeanor and tone changes. She offers to send food and used clothing home with Boyd, suggesting she believes his family is poor, and not at the same social class. It was brilliantly written, and showed overt racism in action. Even as a 7-year old, I recognized the same attitude in my own family, and I chose a different path.

Once you have seen something, you can't un-see it, and it affects how you view the world. What are your biases? Do you know? Do they serve you?

I haven't been able to get rid of all of my biases. I still think the best hockey players in the world are Canadian — and during the playoffs I let it show!

Classroom Exercise

When I first started managing staff, I was told that I had to correct them when they made mistakes. As a rookie manager, I didn't think it was necessary to tell them when they were doing things right. I'd like to say I'm sorry to anyone who worked for me at that time — I'm sure I was a horrible manager.

When I am speaking at conferences, I do an interactive exercise with audience members that show very quickly the effect of praise and criticism and a combination of praise and correction. I send three people out of the room and ask the audience to come up with a task we want each of them to do when they come back. It can be anything from drawing an X on a flipchart, to sitting in a chair. The task itself is not important.

We agree that regardless of what the first participant does, we are going to cheer them. When they walk in, I tell them there is something they need to figure out, that we have something they are supposed to do, and the audience is there to cheer them on. Then, regardless of what they do, the audience cheers. If they move, they are cheered, if they do a dance they are cheered. Some of the participants get quite animated. I've had a few sing a song and do a couple of dance steps. After 60 seconds, I ask them to sit, since they weren't successful in completing the task.

The second person comes in, and again, we tell them they are required to do something and that the audience is going to let them know if they aren't doing it right. If they move, they are booed. If they stand still they are booed. After a long and painful minute, they are asked to sit down. Even though they know this is just an exercise, most of them feel awful when they are booed.

The third person comes in, and is told that they are going to be given encouragement. I don't tell them it will be a combination of cheering and booing, but they figure this out pretty quickly. In every single demonstration, this person is able to discern and carry out what we want them to do, usually in half the time that was allotted. When we are working with our teams, they have to know what they are doing right and wrong. It is only when we combine both that we get things done correctly. In the exercise, I also make sure that the person who was booed gets a standing ovation to undo the awful feeling of being booed in front of a large audience!

Testing for Dishonesty

In another one of professor, Dan Ariely's, experiments on dishonesty, he tested to see if cheating was contagious, and found that dishonesty could be transmitted to others.

What? You can pass on dishonesty like a bad case of the flu? Yes. When cheating was tolerated, and had no consequences, it shaped others' behavior, and cheating increased. It was virally transmitted! The more people who were allowed to get away with cheating, the more others did it too.

Immoral contagion is real, and if we are going to bring more trust to the world, we must demand trustworthy behavior. The good news is that just as negative behavior is contagious, so is honest and moral behavior.

I don't believe that the people at Wells Fargo who opened up accounts without clients knowing were immoral. It was an environment that encouraged dishonest practices, and people were rewarded for cheating, and punished for being honorable. It supported what Ariely discovered in his controlled experiments.

This has a lot of implications for our world. If lying goes unpunished, it proliferates. If you want trustworthy behavior, you have to make sure you know what you are cheering and what you are booing — otherwise you won't get the outcomes you want.

Chapter 11

EXEMPLARS OF THE FIVE
TENETS OF TRUST

I've talked throughout the book about my Five Tenets of Trust, which all start with the letter C. To help you understand how these tenets work in real life, here are some people who exemplify each one.

Commitment: Janice Goodine

When you are committed to something, you go for it with everything you've got. If you make an agreement or promise, you keep it even if it's difficult. Keeping commitments shows integrity.

When I think of commitment and trust at work, I think of my long-time friend, Janice Goodine. She is an Academy Award nominee for her set decorating on the 1993 Academy Award winning movie *Unforgiven*, and a Genie award winner for her work on the movie *Passchendaele*. She has the respect of some of the biggest producers in Hollywood, as much for her character as her impeccable work.

When I was 17, I had a crush on my brother's best friend — well, didn't we all? He had a girlfriend though, and I wanted to get to know her. She was hard to avoid, as they were always hanging out at our house. She had a lot of qualities I didn't like: She was pretty, she tanned, she was talented, she was one of the artistic few who made it into the Alberta College of Art in a very competitive year. She was the youngest in her art classes, and of course, she had the guy.

The more I got to know Janice, though, the more I loved and admired her as a person. As young crushes often go, I quickly got over any feelings I had for Pete and moved on. Jan and I became great friends, and I was one of her bridesmaids when she ended up marrying Pete.

Life Commitments

Janice's mother committed suicide while Jan was in high school, and it had been up to Janice to raise her two little brothers, and keep the household together. That was the situation she was in when she met Pete. She left one difficult situation to land in another.

Unfortunately, Pete turned out to be anything but a catch, and Jan showed her strength when she left the physically abusive relationship, and started raising a young child as a single Mom. When they married she dropped out of school at his insistence, as he wanted her to stay home with the baby. Isolation is a typical move of an abuser.

Jan made the commitment that she would find a way back to her past life. The weeks before she left were scary, since she knew that if he found out, it would result in another beating. I was one of the few people she confided in when she was plotting her escape. Perhaps she found the strength to get through this because life had already thrown her a few curve balls, so she knew life wasn't always fair.

After she left Pete, Jan moved back home temporarily, and took out student loans to go back to school. Trying to juggle a heavy school schedule, parenting, working a job at a retail store, and taking care of the house would have felled many, but she persisted. She was committed to giving her son the best life she could. Being back in the art world, Jan met people who shared the same passions, including John, another artist who was working in the TV industry.

John was in the art department of community television, and Jan often worked for him since she had the talent, intelligence, and aptitude to learn things quickly. The crew loved working with her. John got a big opportunity for a lucrative production, with more status and better pay, and handed in his resignation. The community television station didn't have anyone to take over the position he was leaving, so Jan stepped in. She aced it, and her reputation started to grow as someone who was talented, smart, and good to work with.

Career Commitment

Her big break in the movie industry (it seems in stories like this, there is always a big break) came when she was asked to take over the set decorating on the *Superman* movie — quite a leap from cable television to a big budget movie! The set decorator they had was fired, and they needed someone to step in immediately. Checking around for set decorators in Calgary, they found Jan, and asked her to come for a meeting. She was scared, but she made the commitment to take it on and do a great job. Now she had a big budget, and a union-recognized Hollywood movie under her belt. It was also an opening to begin getting the necessary credits to apply to the Film, Technical, and Crafts Union, which would allow her to play in the big league on a regular basis.

Eight years and many movie credits later, Jan took the step to apply to the union. Membership would mean she could apply for other big movies that were open only to union members.

It was 1986. The head of the union met with her, and told her there was no place in their union for women. He knew they

167

would have to let her in once they vetted her because she had all the necessary credits, but he thought he had found a way around it. He waited until she left Alberta to work on a movie set in Vancouver. The distance between Calgary, Alberta, and Vancouver, British Columbia is 970 km, or over 600 miles. He called her, and told her that the meeting was being held the next day, and if she wanted to be part of the union, she could show up. He also told her it was a one-shot deal. If she didn't show up, she wouldn't be considered again.

She walked into her current boss's office, and told him about the conversation. Without missing a beat, he said, "You're going to that meeting." Thank goodness for people of integrity! He booked her a flight, and the next day Jan showed up at the union meeting. There were 96 men and her — you can imagine the surprise. In spite of the attempts to keep her out, Janice got in. Since that time many, many women have joined that union. Jan opened the door for others. When you are committed to getting things done, you find a way.

In the early-90s, Jan was asked to come to a meeting about a western movie being shot in Alberta. Henry Bumstead was the Production Designer, and Jan thought she was being interviewed for an assistant's position. For those, like me, who didn't know Henry Bumstead's name, he was a well-known Academy Award winning production manager, who worked on some major movies, including *Vertigo, The Sting, To Kill a Mockingbird.* Now, he was working on a western, starring and directed by Clint Eastwood, called *Unforgiven.*

It turned out that Jan wasn't being asked about an assistant's job; she was being hired as the set decorator, with a full crew working under her! She made a commitment that she would be the best-researched and committed set decorator she could be. When she showed up on the set the first day, with her boxes of researched material on the era, and what things would have looked like back then, Henry told her he had never seen better prepared and more researched work. Jan went on to receive the Academy Award nomination for her work.

In case you think that working on a movie is glamorous work, let me describe a day on one movie set she worked on. There were long 12 -14 hour days in cold, wet mud, outside in any and all temperatures. Physically, mentally, and emotionally demanding. There were days when she had to demand clean toilets for her crew, when the porta-potties were disgustingly filled to overflow. It is not the glamorous life most people think of when they think of movie making.

When you are committed, you have the joy of working on great sets with people who trust your vision and treat you well, magic happens, as it did on *Unforgiven*, and again on *Passchendaele*.

Although Jan didn't win an Academy Award for her set decorating on *Unforgiven*, she did receive a Genie Award, Canada's equivalent to the American Oscars, for her set decorating on *Passchendaele*. Any crews who work for Jan know that she looks out for them, and they come to her if they have any problems.

It appears to me, as an outside observer, that the movie industry has allowed abuse to run rampant, and is just now setting some long overdue guidelines. Jan told me the story about a young girl she hired, and how she handled a director with bad intentions. This was back in the early-2000s, way before the *#MeToo* movement. For a moment, I want you to appreciate the power a director has on set. They are virtually omnipotent, and do what they want.

Jan's new hire was pretty, inexperienced, and well-liked by the rest of the team. At the end of the day, she was asked to pick up a prop at the warehouse, which was a short distance from Jan's office, and bring it to the set. A short time later, she came running back in tears. One of the directors on the movie had seen her walk to the warehouse on her own. He followed her, grabbed her, forcibly kissed her, and was forcing himself on her. She managed to fight him off, and ran back to Jan's office, shaking and crying. Jan calmed her down and tried to convince her to lay charges. She refused.

What Jan did next didn't surprise me. She marched into the director's office and said "You ever touch another girl on this set, I will cut off your balls, and hand them to you in a basket." He turned white, since the look on Jan's face told him she wasn't joking.

If you met Jan you'd be hard pressed to find a kinder, gentler person. I've witnessed her saving more baby birds and woodland creatures than Cinderella. But no one should dare to abuse someone on her crew.

Jan said that years later, he saw her on a movie set, and was visibly shaking when he walked up to her and said, "Jan, I don't try anything on the sets. I promise." Obviously he still trusted that she would follow through on her promise if he didn't behave.

With all of her accolades and accomplishments, I asked her what she was proudest of. Without missing a beat, she mentioned her long and happy marriage to her friend and partner, Dean Goodine, and her son, Sean Blackie. Her commitment to both of them is returned by the love and respect they have for one another.

Caring: Dr. Anabel Jensen

When I picture care, I think of Dr. Anabel Jensen, President of *Six Seconds*, an organization dedicated to spreading emotional intelligence around the globe. They are doing a pretty good job of it so far, with offices and representatives in 25 countries, and members in over 167 countries.

You haven't really had a hug until you've had one from Dr. Jensen. She greets everyone she meets with a hug that envelops and draws them in. When I asked her if she would allow me to interview her for my book, I wasn't surprised, but definitely pleased when she said *yes*. In an organization the size and scope of *Six Seconds*, there is always something to attend to, and her time is precious. I told her that when I thought about the first tenet of caring, her face was the one I saw, since she exemplifies caring in action.

When you care about someone, you demonstrate that through your actions and words. It entails listening wholeheartedly and without judgment. When you care about someone, you notice things about them. You are in tune with how they feel, and take an interest in what interests them.

When I asked Dr. Jensen what we could do to increase care, she answered, "At the end of the day I ask myself these questions:

- Did I bring joy and laughter to one person today?
- Did I practice empathy?
- Did I help the environment today?
- Did I take care of the dog today?
- Did I ask for feedback?

Some days, the only question I can answer in the affirmative is, Did I take care of the dog today?"

A lover of Benjamin Franklin, Dr. Jensen said he was the first person to write a self-help journal, and much of it had to do with integrating small acts, on a daily basis, to increase care.

A *Noble Goal* is something *Six Seconds* teaches, defining it as a goal that can't be achieved in our lifetime.

Noble Goals Definition: "Connecting your daily choices with your overarching sense of purpose.

Importance: **Noble Goals** activate all the other competencies in the **Six Seconds** Model of EQ. ... Having a clear **Noble Goal** helps you focus on what is most important, and access your full power and potential."

Dr. Jensen's *Noble Goal* is about integrity, and the balance between ability and compassion. She also wants to help others reach their own Noble Goal. Here is how she describes hers: "I will teach accountability and compassion, so that ethical decisions will flood the earth."

The first time I heard about the *Noble Goal* concept was at a *Six Seconds* workshop. I have to admit, I couldn't imagine working with the business community, and talking to them about *Noble Goals*. It didn't sound like something the business people I knew would even listen to.

The more I worked with the concept, the more I could see how powerful it was in directing and focusing people to do work that had meaning. It certainly makes me understand why I think of Dr. Jensen when I think of the tenet of Caring. She cares deeply about people and the world.

Dr. Jensen lives in an interesting world, since she teaches, breathes, and lives with a world of emotional intelligence. The challenge is to be emotionally intelligent, and still help people to grow. It isn't always easy, because being honest and giving feedback can feel uncomfortable. She does it by modeling openness and vulnerability, and seeks insights by asking people she knows well, "What do I do that annoys you?"

She believes we lack insight about ourselves. We really don't know ourselves as well as we could. "Feedback," says Dr. Jensen, "is like a piece of popcorn. No matter what, even if you disagree with 99.9% of it, there is still .1% of it that will be of benefit to you." What is the kernel that will help you to grow as a person?

Trust is built on self-trust, and you need a small group of individuals, family members or non-family members, who will give you feedback — the kind of feedback you get when you ask, "What do I do that annoys you?" These are the people who will give you their compassionate honesty. We can get so stuck in our own biases, that when we have others we can trust to give us another perspective, we are able to make the necessary adjustments.

At the end of our conversation, Dr. Jensen talked about a young niece, who had lived with her for a year. Dr. Jensen's family asked for her help because of emotional issues her niece was going through. By the end of the year, her niece had turned things around. She was accepted at most of the universities she applied to, and was doing amazing work. Her parents asked, "Anabel, what did you do?"

Anabel's answer was, "I just gave her unconditional love. We need people in our lives who love us unconditionally."

Consistency: Michael Kerr

Consistency is being able to achieve a level of performance that does not vary greatly in quality over time. It is also matching words and deeds so that what you say and do align; or what you say is consistent from one day to the other.

I've long admired my friend, Michael Kerr, who is one of the top speakers and humorists in Canada. He has achieved the highest honors and designations the speaking industry grants, as one of a few to achieve his CSP (Certified Speaking Professional) and HOF (Hall of Fame).

I don't know how he does it, time after time, being able to go out on stage and get people laughing while they learn, and consistently receiving accolades and recommendations when he speaks. It's a tough business, and you are often at the mercy of circumstances you can't control.

You may have a room where the audience is uncomfortable, and can't see or hear you as well as they should; or it could be an audience that is hostile because of news from their company, or an after-dinner crowd that has imbibed too much, and just wants to keep on partying. Michael has had them all, and time after time he delivers.

Michael knows that when a new client calls, there is a lot on the line. The client's reputation will be judged on how well he does. They are also paying a lot of money. He starts building trust before he even speaks to the client. On his website, he writes that *his* goal is to help *them* achieve their goals, and if they decide he's not the right fit, he'll recommend someone else. Michael has been in the business long enough to know that aligning their needs with his skills is important for them both, and asks questions that uncovers potential problems the client may not have thought of.

He looks at what is best for the client, and communicates that. The 17 pages of testimonials on his website show that he consistently delivers.

Here are some things I learned from Michael about matching actions with promises:

- Be responsive. When a client calls with a question, answer as soon as you possibly can, **every time**.
- Be aware of unspoken communication. If you are working with someone who is micromanaging, they may have fears that need to be addressed. Be brave, and have the difficult conversations, **every time**.
- Realize that things can go wrong, and have a plan in place so you know what to do, **every time**
- Know what the client's expectations are, and take the extra steps to exceed them, **every time**

- Communicate, communicate, communicate. Ask probing questions your clients might not have thought of, **every time**.

I do believe that Michael has a talent for *finding the funny* (as he calls it) in almost any situation, but his skills on stage are the result of consistent practice and hard work. He is one of the top humorists in Canada, because he's shown that he can be trusted to do what he says he will do.

Competence: Brent Darnell

Brent Darnell is the personification of **Competence,** the ability to do something successfully or efficiently.

Brent teaches soft skills in a hard industry — construction. He is listened to because he has shown he has the competence and experience to understand what they are dealing with. He's tried bringing in other experts, but if they don't have construction experience, they are often dismissed.

A mutual friend referred me to Brent in 2002, when he needed emotional intelligence experts to debrief a group of Senior Leaders of a construction company he was working with. Since that time, I've watched as Brent received the highest honors for his work in transforming the construction industry's Alpha Males. (He also works with women in the construction industry, but the problems they face are different.)

In an industry that is still predominantly male, and the environments are hyper masculine, stressful, and have no tolerance for vulnerability, it's not surprising that the Center for Disease Control found that construction has some of the highest suicide rates of any industry — 80% higher than most medical professionals, air traffic controllers, or employees in protective services, such as fireman or policemen.

175

When Brent is talking to a new group, the first slide he shows is a picture of his father as a young man, working on a construction site. He tells them he is a third generation construction guy, and he's worked in almost every job imaginable. He started out as the *go-for*, running errands, moving up to wielding a hammer, and ending as the construction engineer, managing the sites. He's seen and done it all.

I wanted to know what Brent said and did to get the tough guys to listen, accept, and use what he was offering. My Dad was in construction, and I was trying to imagine him and his crew listening to someone talk about emotional intelligence. All I could imagine was laughter and derision.

Brent meets them where they are, without forcing change. No judgments. He listens to find out who they are, and what they are trying to achieve, and acknowledges that he has felt the same. Wherever they are, that is where he starts.

He described two groups of twelve superintendents he worked with, that were the roughest, toughest guys you could imagine. They told Brent straight up, "I don't care if someone on the crew is going through a divorce. They need to leave that crap at home."

He asks them if they would be interested in how they could achieve better results, with a lot less wear and tear on them during the day. They get that. He goes on to let them know that he's going to show them a different set of skills to get better performance with less stress. They already have the driving part of the job down really well; these are skills I would call the social emotional skills of leadership.

Brent went on to tell me the story of John.

"John was sent to me when he was moved off a project because of his difficult relationship with the men who reported to him. He was a 50-year old superintendent, and when I first met him, he looked like a whipped dog. He was devastated that he had been fired from that project.

"He felt awful, and didn't understand why it happened. He said he drove them because he cared so much for all of them, and wanted them to succeed. He wanted everyone to be the very best they could be, and believed that driving them was the best way to achieve that goal."

Brent empathized with John, telling him he had been there himself. He told him he wasn't there to fix him, because he wasn't broken. Then he showed him another way of looking at the issue.

"You're pretty awesome the way you are, but people don't understand your approach. What if we gave you a different set of tools? That's all this is. You're a smart guy. You can learn these tools, and then you'll be able to get better results."

Brent could say this because he really has been there. He knows what it's like to work with tough guys with performance issues. You can drive them, write letters to their company, hold their money, do all kinds of punitive things, but it gets limited results. When you take the time to find out what is really going on, then you can solve the problems. You can't solve the problem if you don't know what it is.

John got on board. With Brent's competence and guidance, he improved his empathy and self-awareness skills dramatically. He also worked on getting more balance between his assertiveness and his empathy.

Within six months, his company put him on a new project with a very difficult client. They felt so comfortable with what he learned, they were willing to give him one of the tougher assignments. The representative for the construction management firm he reported was being irrational, unreasonable, and staged issues that he reported to the owner.

John was able to handle this difficult situation because of his newfound ability to get along with his team and the owner's representative. He did so well that they ended up firing the construction management firm, and worked directly with John's company. Within ten months, he was promoted to operations manager for one of his company's larger geographic areas.

Sometimes the skills that improve relationships at work improve relationships at home. Six months after the work between Brent and John had finished, Brent got a call for help. John said, "I know you're not a counselor, but I need your advice." He trusted Brent's competence in being able to see all sides of the situation. Brent confirmed that he wasn't a counselor, but said if he could help with something that didn't cross the line into therapy, he'd be happy to hear him out.

John told him that his niece had moved into his home and, without mincing words, said he and his wife really disliked her, and that she was a major pain in the butt. She was angry all the time, and was trying to tell them what to do.

Brent asked, "What's happening with her?" John told him she had just gone through a divorce, and then lost her job. She had nowhere to go, and no way to support herself, so they let her move in with them. Now they were seriously thinking of throwing her out. Brent asked him if he remembered how he felt the first time they talked.

John's mouth dropped open. He recognized that how his niece was feeling now was the same way he felt when he first heard from Brent. He hadn't thought of it in this way. He recognized that she probably felt really bad about herself, and told Brent he was going to call a family meeting. The family meeting was about getting everyone to show that they cared and supported her as she was going through this.

Two weeks later he called Brent back to tell him about the miracle. As soon as the family had the talk with his niece, everything changed; She got a job, she started dating someone, and felt good about herself. True care and love made all the difference.

I know a lot of Brent's success is because he cares deeply about others as much as his competence and ability to share his processes and skills.

Communication: The Tenet They all have in common

Dr. Anabel Jensen, Janice Goodine, Michael Kerr, and Brent Darnell all share a common skill. They are able to communicate through words and actions that they can be trusted.

The one thing they do better than most people I have met is listening. You know those people who listen to you so they can respond with their own brilliant answer? I've caught myself preparing my answer, even before the person has finished talking, and I'm working on listening whole-heartedly. They listen with their whole hearts and you can feel all five of the Tenets in action.

It's important to communicate that you care by listening deeply, and responding thoughtfully. Be consistent in your message, committed to communicate not once, but until there is understanding and competence in how you word the message.

All these people are extremely competent, and willing to admit when they don't know. When you are confident, you don't need to pretend you know something you don't, or pretend to be someone you're not.

Chapter 12

BRINGING TRUST TO LIFE

I hope all the stories I've told throughout the book have illustrated the fact that this is not just theory. Trust is real, and it affects our lives in many ways, both good and bad. In this chapter, I bring together some reflections and stories that underline the practical aspects of trust in life.

The Longest Flight Home

Since I grew up experiencing Canadian winters, you'd think I'd know that Converse sneakers with no socks aren't good in the snow. But then, I wasn't expecting snow in late September.

I was flying home from Calgary, Alberta to Philadelphia, Pennsylvania. The morning of my flight, I woke up to two feet of snow. It had been beautiful the previous day, with people in short sleeved shirts, enjoying the last vestiges of a glorious fall. I knew it was hot and sunny in Philadelphia, so I dressed for where I was traveling to, and not where I was leaving from.

Because of the unexpected bad weather, I left for the airport almost two hours early. I knew traffic could be a nightmare on the freeway, and wanted to give myself plenty of time to get there and return the rental car. It seems to be a law of the universe that if you plan for something, the opposite will happen. Traffic was light, I breezed through the return line, up at the car rental, checked my bag, and got through security in record time.

I arrived at the gate in plenty of time for the earlier flight. Since I checked my bag, I didn't have the option of switching. That flight left on time, so I was surprised when they said my flight was going to be delayed because of the snow. I had a two-hour window to make my connecting flight, so I wasn't too worried.

When we were finally able to board the plane, that two-hour window shrunk to less than one hour — still no cause for concern. The pilot came on, and told us we were second in line for de-icing, a procedure that sprays a solution on the wings that prevents ice from forming, so the plane can safely take off.

Then we sat for five hours. Ugh. Once the doors are closed you are not allowed to get off the plane.

My friend, Jeannie Cockell, is one of the world experts in Appreciative Inquiry, and I learned from her to ask myself this question in situations that are less than ideal: "What is there to appreciate?" For me it was making connections with others. The women across from me were supposed to speak at a conference that afternoon; the fellow behind me was a recruiter for the National Hockey League, going up to view a game, and the gentleman next to me was a senior vice president going to a meeting.

It seemed like most of the people had urgent meetings to get to, while my speaking engagement back in Pennsylvania was a couple of days away. Out of all of us sharing information and talking, I had the easiest time of it, since I had a one-day buffer. If you've flown enough, you know that eventually the law of averages will catch up to you, and you'll have a bad flying day. Clearly, this was mine.

Most of the people on the plane were making the best of the situation, but there was one person who decided he should be the spokesperson to let the cabin crew know how abysmally they were failing at their job, and how horrible the airline was. For more than two hours, he ranted. It was when he said that any airline that was run this poorly was not safe, and all of our lives were in danger, that most of us shushed him, and asked him to tone it down. His next comment was that most people weren't bright enough to recognize what he was able to recognize. That got a chuckle.

For new travelers, this was enough to make their already awful trip truly frightening, so I was happy when the group was able to silence him. It was, after all, a flight filled with mostly Canadians, and in this instance, we earned our reputation for being polite. Many of us recognized that the very pleasant, young flight attendant didn't know how to deal with this vocally irate customer.

Here are some things she could have done:

- First, recognize that his anger may be covering up his fear. Anger is a powerful emotion, and for many people it makes them feel more in control than giving in to their fear. Angry people are hard to reason with, because their ability to think clearly is impaired. They are experiencing an amygdala hijack, and their emotions are overpowering their reason.

- Don't take it personally. It's not about you, so don't add fuel to the emotional firestorm by adding your anger.

- Listen. Look at them, and hear them out. Even if they are spouting misinformation, let them speak. Don't interrupt, and tell them they are wrong. Repeat back to them what they have said. Show them you heard what they were upset about.

- Give them time. In this situation, the passenger needed to calm down. Showing him that he had been heard, telling him she was getting information, and then coming back to quietly talk to him would have given him time to disengage, without telling him to calm down, which usually inflames the situation.

- Apologize gracefully. In this instance, it was not the airline's fault, but telling that to the customer would have made the matter worse. "I'm so sorry that you have to be on the plane so long." Sometimes using humor can diffuse the situation, as long as the customer doesn't feel they are being mocked." I know all of us could have walked there by now" might have worked!

- Offer them something. Although this customer kept asking for an alcoholic drink, the flight attendant wisely chose to instead offer him tea, coffee, or a soft drink.

- Finally, take a moment to process your own feelings.

I Can Tell the Whole World, But I Can't Tell You

Flipping through the TV channels, I was intrigued by what I saw on the screen. With tears streaming from her eyes, the woman turned slowly, looked at the man sitting across from her, and with encouragement from television's *can fix everything in an hour shrink*, Dr. Phil, she told her partner she wasn't happy, and was going to be leaving him. What? She waited until she was on national TV to have this intimate conversation? She could tell the whole world, but couldn't find the words to tell it in private? I've always found these scenarios uncomfortable and kind of fake, but I see a similar soap opera playing out in the boardroom again and again.

Scenes from the Boardroom

Bob, the manager, gathered everyone together, and told them it had come to his attention that people were coming in late, which was causing morale problems in the office. His steely stare made eye contact with everyone in the room. Jaws jutted, eyes narrowed and mumbling under their breath, they returned the intense stare. The problem of lateness wasn't a big one. Most of the staff consistently arrived early to start the day, and stayed late to get work done.

Out of the two people who were late, Alice was a single parent with the usual things to be done to get out the door. She made arrangements through the Human Resources department to have a later start time to accommodate dropping her child off at daycare. She more than made up for it in her productivity, and the work she took home.

Alice put in extra time working at home to complete projects late at night when her child was in bed. Every review was stellar, and the caliber of her work was exceptional.

If Bob had only taken the time to talk to his staff he would have known this.

Bob was new to the job, desperately wanted to show his authority, and have people respect him. A bit of research might have made a difference in the decision to hold the meeting, especially for Alice.

Hearing Bob talk about the problem of lateness, without identifying who it was directed to was demoralizing to Alice. She was distracted for the rest of the day, and worried about her future with the company. Part of the day was spent on recruiting websites, looking for new job opportunities. Alice knew that with her specialized skills, and work ability, finding another company wasn't going to be difficult, but she worried about getting the late start that was so important to her and her son.

The one person the whole talk was actually directed to had no reason for their lateness, other than he hated getting up in the mornings. But now, he felt reassured, since he believed lateness was a common problem, and didn't feel the talk was directed solely at him. He thought that the 15 minutes he was late everyday wasn't a big deal, because no one had said anything to him directly.

In my coaching work with managers, most say they hate confrontation, and it is easier to give negative feedback to a group than talk to the person who is the problem. It hits on two areas of distrust.

1. **They didn't trust their ability to handle conflict**
2. **They didn't trust the employee to handle the feedback.**

The problems this caused were greater than the problem of one employee being late. The rest of the staff felt their efforts weren't appreciated, and they resented being admonished for a problem they didn't contribute to. Productivity suffered. Morale suffered, and the manager lost trust.

Bring in the Five Tenets of Trust

In the Five Tenets of Trust, **Caring** shows up in the friendly tone, the smile, and people engaging in open and honest communication.

Believing that everyone cheers for the same team puts you at a disadvantage. Taking time to get to know people, and showing them you care enough to learn who they are and what's important to them can make a difference, especially if you are the leader.

When I've asked participants in a workshop to give me a behavior that shows caring in action, inevitably someone mentions loyalty. What loyalty means to them is knowing that the person will defend them when they are not present, will make good on their word, and will handle confidential information with care and discretion.

Rambling on and on, as our new manager did, ensures that people will tune out, or be unsure of what is wanted. Knowing what you want them to understand before you speak helps to hone your message and get to the point.

Commitment is important, and our new manager certainly had the right to expect people to show up. Recognize what commitment looks like.

When a group or team is committed, they speak passionately about the goal, and take ownership of their part in achieving it. On an individual level, you'll see them show up on time and share information with others. You'll see them wanting to put their personal mark on their work.

Here are some reasons people may not make a commitment to their work:

- Lack of accountability. The credit for their work isn't given to them — ever, and no one notices when they do great work.
- Fear of retribution. Mistakes are punished, which stifles creative thinking.
- No shared vision. People don't know what they are supposed to commit to.
- No idea of how success is measured. They have no way to know if they have succeeded.
- A demand for group think. This is to the detriment of everyone as individuals.
- A bullying workplace or an antagonistic member. He or she is allowed to run roughshod over others.

Consistency shows in myriad ways. How can a manager say he trusts his staff, but tries to micromanage? The two are inconsistent. Words and behavior have to align.

Think about the moody coworker who has such a mercurial nature, that you never know from one day to the next how they will show up; or how about the work an employee does that is great one day, but not the next. We trust others when we know what to expect of them.

The one tenet that needs to constantly change to stay the same is **competence**! Having the skills to do your job requires you to stay abreast of what is happening in the world. There aren't too many jobs that don't require to you to be a lifelong learner. Everything from gardening to geophysics changes, and in order for others to trust you, you need to stay aware of what is happening in your field. As a manager, are you providing your staff with opportunities to learn and grow as individuals, and in their field?

What if our manager had taken the time to learn about the people on his team? What if he worked on communicating with each of his staff?

Communication is more than opening your mouth and having words come out. It isn't communication until the other person understands what you are telling them.

The best communicators are excellent listeners. According to neuroscientist, Dr. David Rock, you must allow people to think through their own issues, rather than telling them what to do or what to think. You can ask questions that help them think about their thinking. Here are questions you can ask:

- How can I best help you think this through?
- When you say you're not sure about ____, which part do you want to discuss with me?
- How much has this been on your mind?
- How can I best help you with your thinking?

No one likes talking to someone who appears to be listening, only so that they can make their point. Don't just listen to respond, listen to understand and appreciate.

If Bob watched the response of the staff when he was talking about lateness, he would have noticed the eye rolls, and the clamped jaws of the audience. A large part of communication is reading the nonverbal signals.

Making eye contact is important, but don't overdo it, and know what it means when you're getting the penetrating stare. The manager may have believed that the intense eye contact meant they were engaged with what he was saying, but research shows the opposite. When people feel threatened, intense eye contact is, sometimes, an aggressive maneuver to dominate. Context is important!

Dr. Albert Mehrabian is professor emeritus of Psychology at UCLA. In 1970, he created his model of communication, which showed how important body language and tone were in face-to-face communication. Imagine someone yelling and stomping their feet, while they are saying "I'm not angry." Would you believe the words they were saying, or what you were seeing and hearing? As I said, context is important.

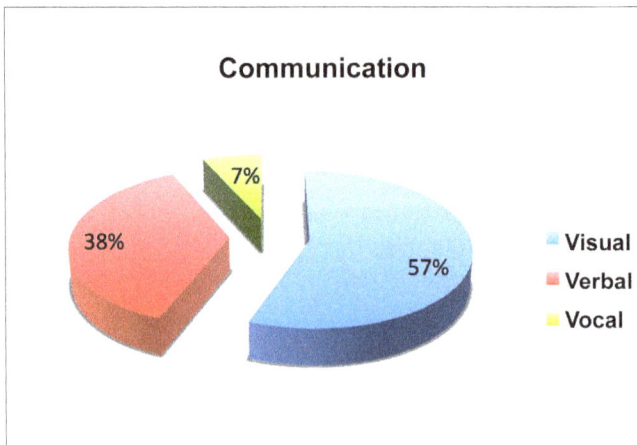

Communication

- Visual 57%
- Verbal 38%
- Vocal 7%

Using the Five Tenets

For Heather Peace, of Superior Contact in Marquette, Michigan, the light bulb moment happened in a workshop of mine she attended in Orlando, Florida, at the ICMI leadership conference. ICMI is the leading industry expert for improving contact center efficiency, and every year they have a conference offering call center managers' workshops with experts like myself.

Heather is highly trusted by her team, and she searches for ways to make them and her company better.

At the ICMI workshop were 60 middle and senior leaders, from contact centers across North America. In all my time training, I can't remember a more attentive and engaged group.

Heather's style is very much hands-off. She spends a lot of time hiring competent staff, and believes that they are in the role because they have the skills, and she is there to support them, not over manage them.

Her ah-ha moment came when I asked participants to discuss a segment of TRUSTED, in which the protagonist, Hunter, doesn't show up to a meeting he called, and can't understand why his team is upset.

Heather remembers sitting in the group and thinking, "Well he probably had a really good reason." Not being a fan of meetings herself, she listened to others in the workshop who shared different perspectives and Heather had an epiphany. She cancelled meetings, believing her team would be grateful for the time it freed up. What if the opposite was true?

When she returned to her office, she decided to make meetings a regular weekly occurrence. Instead of seeing them as a waste of time, she used them as opportunities to get to know her team better, to share goals and expectations, and find out what they needed on a regular basis.

Heather introduced the Five Tenets of Trust to her team, and refers to them throughout the week. When a new hire was having difficulty, she spent time showing that she was committed to her success, and met with her on a daily basis to go over what her tasks were, and make sure she understood. Through her actions, she shows them she cares about their success. She makes sure her staff understands that the corporate culture is to support, evolve, and elevate all of them, and lets them know what they need to do in order to be successful.

One of her initiatives, after my workshop, was to conduct a job-shadowing group to help people understand how their jobs fit into the overall success of the company. It was completely voluntary, and the customer service representatives were allowed off the phone to join her for a casual interactive presentation.

It helped them to understand the different roles in the company, what the key performance indicators were, who their clients were, and finally, a review of how the Five Tenets — caring, commitment, consistency, competence, and communication — showed up in the way they trusted each other.

"It was really great watching them interact and see them realize why the metrics and targets were so important. They saw me as someone who wants them to succeed, rather than a person who looks for mistakes." said Heather. Now, Heather also takes calls so she can understand what her agents go through.

Heather said, "Now when I walk out on the floor, people are communicating with me. They aren't turning away. They've discovered I'm not this scary manager. In fact, one of the agents told me that she wanted me to know that she trusted me one hundred percent".

"It's a really, really tough job to be on the phone some days. We tell them to make sure they have a smile in their voice when they are talking to people. But sometimes the agents are getting yelled at over and over again on the calls. Being able to talk to them and their supervisors, and letting them know you care and understand goes a long way. So does telling them to go for a break or sometimes springing for pizza as a show of appreciation."

Doing these extra steps to incorporate trust has made Heather and her team a happier, more productive group. I believe it will do the same for any leader who wants to build a trusted workplace, full of loyal employees who are assets to the organization.

In Closing

When I was younger, I believed that people who were successful were living easier lives than I was.

Now, I know that isn't true. Sometimes it is the exact opposite. Our strength to tackle life's challenges with trust and determination comes from learning and growing through our challenges, and staying kind, open, and honest in spite of them.

When we are able to show others how much we care for them, by listening without judgment, *we add to trust.* When we see ourselves with unclouded eyes, and accept, care, and love ourselves *we increase trust.* When we open ourselves to the help that is out there, and are willing to be vulnerable, *we build trust.* With more trust comes wisdom. It helps guide us to be the best we can be for the world. It is my hope that we are able to increase our trust from wherever it currently sits.

With trust and hope,

Lea

About the Author

Lea Brovedani is an author and sought after speaker who is one of North America's leading experts on trust. She has been named Top Thought Leaders on Trust for 2017, 2018 and 2019 by the organization Trust Across America.

She is also the author of TRUSTED – Secret Lessons from an Inspired Leader, a contributing author in four other books and Lea continues to share her expertise in business magazines around the world.

Globally recognized, Lea has worked in numerous industry sectors and in numerous countries including Canada, USA, Europe, Singapore, Africa and Indonesia. She has developed training programs and workshops that focus on more productive and profitable workforces through leadership strategies that increase efficacy in communication and trust.

The Optimized Workforce Engagement Strategy is Lea's proprietary leadership program that cultivates stronger and more solid leaders by improving their trustworthiness.

This proven approach builds a more satisfied workforce and creates a more positive customer experience for the client. In turn, with an increase in confidence between all stakeholders the outcome builds a more profitable bottom line for the organization.

Optimize your workforce or next event by contacting Lea Brovedani *lea@leabrovedani.com*.

Index

www.ingramcontent.com/pod-product-compliance
Lightning Source LLC
Chambersburg PA
CBHW060543210326
41519CB00014B/3332